Marina Al

WISE TALES FOR CHILDREN AND ADULTS

First copy to most loyal and charming member of Guido — BELA KOGAN.

From publisher

Mount Arutdjewr

12/05/2024

Prize of Maria Shevel for the best Children's book
London 2024

Published by Hertfordshire Press Ltd © 2024
e-mail: publisher@hertfordshirepress.com
www.hertfordshirepress.com

WISE TALES FOR CHILDREN AND ADULTS

by Marina Alyassova ©

English

Translated by Jonathan Campion
Illustrations by Véronika Zaleskaya—veronika.schrigen
& Irina Shishkanova
Design by Alexandra Rey

British Library Catalogue in Publication Data
A catalogue record for this book is available from the British Library
Library of Congress in Publication Data
A catalogue record for this book has been requested

ISBN: 978-1-913356-83-5

Prize of Maria Shevel
for the best Children's book

In 2016, Hertfordshire Press took the initiative of establishing a special prize for the best work written for children of the Open Eurasia literary contest (also known as OEBF*), thereby underscoring the significance of children's literature. We are grateful to this prize for enabling wonderful books from children's writers, professional psychologists and devoted mothers from Azerbaijan, Yakutia, the USA, Russia, Kyrgyzstan and Uzbekistan to be published.

The prize was named in honour of Maria Shevel, an architect who made a significant contribution to the development of the Hungry Steppe (Uzbekistan) and a mother of five children who was duly recognised with a number of state awards. A number of other honours were bestowed upon her, including Hero of Labour, Veteran of Labour, Medal of Motherhood and many others. Maria Shevel was born on 1 May 1943 in the Sumy region of Ukraine. Following her graduation from the Institute, she was assigned to Central Asia, where she contributed to the construction of the Toktogul hydroelectric power station in Kyrgyzstan. Since 1965, she had the privilege of working under the personal supervision of Sharaf Rashidov on the development of the Hungry Steppe and the architectural appearance of the city of Jizzak (Uzbekistan). Her example of dedication to life and work continues to inspire her children and grandchildren, who live in Uzbekistan, Russia, Poland and the UK.

Hertfordshire Press (UK) is a distinctive British publishing house that strives to bridge the gap between English-speaking readers and Eurasia through the publication of books, magazines, and guidebooks by authors from the region. We are happy to be able to offer authors the opportunity to have their work published in 12 different languages. We are pleased to be able to offer our books in both hard copy and electronic versions.

Since 2002, the publishing house has been focusing on the publication of modern fiction and popular scientific literature by Eurasian authors, as well as the republication of works from previous years which are not currently available in English. We are proud to share that our catalogue contains over 250 works by authors from 17 countries, with a total print run of over 1,000,000 copies.

The Open Eurasian Literature Festival & Book Forum (OEBF) is a distinctive annual event that plays a unique role in promoting Eurasian literature on an international scale. As a cultural bridge between East and West, it offers a valuable platform for authors and artists to engage in dialogue about their work, share experiences and connect with like-minded individuals from diverse countries, fostering potential collaborations.

Please don't hesitate to contact us
publisher@ocamagazine.com
or visit our website at www.eng.awardslondon.com
or www.eurasiancreativeguild.uk.

Love is always an activity, not a passive effect.
It is a state of constant–staying- rather than–falling in-.
In the most general sense, the active nature of love
can be described by the statement that to love
means giving first, not taking.

Erich Fromm. The Art of Loving.

PREFACE

The book "Wise Tales for Children and Adults" by coach and psychologist Marina Alyassova is one of the most unpretentious and most important books I have read. The main thing to know about this book is: the tales in it are for children, but the book is also for adults. And there is no contradiction in that. Marina Alyassova's book is in its own way a textbook of mental literacy.

At first glance, everything is really uncomplicated. It is a small collection of very kind stories about a five-year-old girl, Nastenka, and her mother, and each story is a conversation, where Nastenka asks a difficult question, and her mother shares with her daughter worldly wisdom. That's how many informative children's books are structured, isn't it?

But it is the content of these conversations and the questions the little girl asks her mother that make the book so special. You will not find here any academic information that Nastenka will not be able to get at school one day. The girl is not concerned with why the wind blows or moss grows. She comes to her mother with questions about her own feelings and emotions, the behavior of other people and the differences in other people's characters. Nastenka is interested in what is trust, how love manifests itself, why there is sadness or fear, and how to understand the person she does not like. The most difficult questions, the answers to which adults are looking for sometimes all their lives. Or maybe they just did not ask them in time? When they were children, their world was simpler, and it was much more important to understand its laws.

I'm a writer myself, I'm a mother myself. And while everyone reads books differently, I would like to recommend a way to read this particular book. It should be read to an adult first. And then put it aside and read it aloud to a child. Not straight after, or the child will get confused. But exactly at those moments when the child themself faces the situations described in the book, and you need to draw his attention to them, explain them and teach him how to cope with them.

In the first minute the book will seem a little naive and in some places lusciously affectionate. The mother is too wise and perfect, and Nastenka is too smart and obedient. But I assure you—it's not for nothing. Notice the yeast on which the unlikely-ideal relationship between mother and daughter is mixed: on complete trust. The only ingredient that can create true intimacy between people.

Her mother never dismisses her daughter, does not consider her questions silly, and the girl herself is too young to discuss complicated matters with her. That is why Nastenka is attentive to her emotions, looking for names for them and ways to manage them– the very skill that so many of us so catastrophically lack in life. After all, once we heard that "men do not cry", that "you will understand when you grow up", that "you are too young to think about silly things" and that "get a grip, she decided to feel sorry for herself!".

But we grew up and didn't realize it. We forbade ourselves to think about silly things, to feel sorry for ourselves, to cry, but sometimes we still can't pull ourselves together. And now psychologists teach us, already adults, tired, hardened and distrustful, what our own parents should have taught us as children.

But they couldn't, because they weren't taught either. It's such a simple chain.

Nastenka will not always be this sweet child. She will become a teenager, she too will grow needles, she too will be angry at the world, at her mother, at herself. But armed with boundless trust in her mother and a carefully nurtured ability to understand herself and others, she will hardly collapse into the thresher of emotions and fears, doubts and resentments that so many teenagers go through. She will be protected from the bitterest teenage nightmare– "I am not loved and not understood, and probably it is deserved". And the girl's mom will most likely avoid that hurtful cry of "Stay out of this, you won't understand anything anyway, you'll just yell again!" and the slamming of the door.

As you introduce this book into your daily routine, you will notice that very soon you will take Nastenka's mother's experience and begin to make up these kinds of stories for your child according to his or her own questions and personality. If you both like it, you will soon develop a new bond between you that is much more trusting and warm.

Of course, there is no universal experience, no magic advice, no flawless methodology. But "Wise Tales for Children and Adults" is a gentle and uncomplicated way to both strengthen your trusting relationship with your child, and in time to give him invaluable skills to understand himself and others, the ability to ask the right questions and correctly search for answers, to solve conflicts without infringing on their feelings and desires, and to perceive problems proportionately.

It all sounds like a whole psychology textbook. But it's not. They're just stories. Short, kind and very simple. And their only secret is that you need to learn mental literacy from childhood.

Nina Yagolnitzer, writer,
Israel

Wise tales for children and adults

Marina Alyassova

Chapter one

LOVE YOURSELF

Love your neighbor as yourself Matthew 22 37-40

– Mom, what does it mean to love yourself?– climbing on her knees and wrapping herself in her mother's warm arms, little Nastenka asked.

– Where did you hear that?– Mom asked, slightly surprised by her daughter's question.

– Yesterday my grandmother was reading some book called the Bible. So she was talking about the commandments that God had given to people. The first one is to love God, and the second one, Grandma said, is to love your neighbor as yourself. What do you mean, love yourself? Is it to be fed candy and do whatever you want and not deny yourself anything?

Mom laughed and stroked her daughter's head:

– Well, you could say that! That too. But seriously, loving yourself isn't easy.

– Why is it not easy?– Nastenka was surprised.– In our kindergarten teachers love themselves very much. They always keep half of the cake for two people, and share the other half with all the kids.

The mother hesitated at first, not knowing how to respond to her daughter's words. Then she replied:

– Well, they don't like themselves very much– so many sweets at one time! It's bad for your teeth, and it can make you sick.

– Nastenka thought for a few minutes. Her mother watched her daughter's thought process unfold.

– So, if I eat a lot of sweets, it means that I don't like myself?– Nastenka thought aloud.– And then how do I know that I love myself?

Her mother realized that simple phrases would not do the trick, so she decided to talk to her daughter seriously. After all, she is no longer a little girl, she recently turned five. And as long as the child has curiosity, it is important to quench this curiosity, like a thirst. So that there is no unpleasant aftertaste.

– To love yourself, my daughter, is first of all not to harm yourself. For example, when a person is offended and does not speak about his offense, but carries it in himself, this offense begins to destroy him from inside. Such a small worm appears and bites, bites, bites a man, and he becomes even sadder or even more silent, or even more evil. And hatred to the offender sprouts in the person. This is how the second toothy worm appears.

– It hurts when you get bit! I remember my grandfather's dog bit me once. My arm hurt for a week!

– So imagine that this pain can live with a person all his life. And then it turns into a jewel for him, without which he can't live without. And if he loses it, he'll resent himself. And he will start eating himself like a worm.

Nastenka gave it some serious thought.

– So resenting others and yourself is hurting yourself. What should I do, mom? Because Mishka teases me sometimes, and I can't answer him, so I sit in the corner, pouting my lips, until the teacher pulls him away from me. That means I sit there and hurt myself, right?

– It turns out that way,– Mom said, holding her gently against her and slowly stroking her head.– You know, if Mishka teases you, it means that he probably wants to play with you, but he doesn't know how to say it. He hasn't learned yet. He knows how to play with boys, but not with girls. Before you decide whether to take offense or not, you can ask him why he's doing it. You might get him to think about it. And if he doesn't, you shouldn't take offense. Probably, he himself does not really know what he is doing and why.

– Mom– said Nastenka,– I've decided that I'm not going to re- sent Mishka now. Why do I need to grow a biting worm in me? I'd rather play with dolls. They certainly won't do anything bad to me.

– Dolls won't do, that's right,– Mom smiled.

– But people are not dolls,– Nastenka suddenly realized.– What should we do with them then, Mom?

– The most precious jewel you have is yourself,– answered the mother.– And it is important to remember that always. And the way you treat yourself, people will treat you the same way. If you do not respect yourself, others will not respect you. If you are often angry and sad, others will help you in this– they will do everything to make you angry and sad. When the sun shines in your heart and a smile shines on your face, people around you will also smile. They are reacting to your state of mind.

Mom hugged Nastenka even tighter and looked into her eyes. – Oh, Mom, your eyes are smiling!– Mom laughed, and Nastenka smiled too.

– You see, eyes can smile too! And the eyes are the mirror of the soul. If there is light in them, it pleases not only you, but the whole world.

– I got it, Mommy!– Nastenka exclaimed, hugging her moth- er's neck tightly.– I will always smile now, so that a tree of light and goodness will grow in my heart! And I will love myself with this light and goodness! And when I can do that, then I will be able to hug anyone who is near me with that light and goodness, won't I, Mommy?

– The truth, my girl! What you carry inside you, you give to the world. If it's evil and hate, it's evil and hate. If it's love and light, it's love and light. What you choose is up to you. No one is in control. Even God does not interfere in the decisions of His devotees.

That night Nastenka had a wonderful dream, as if she was walking through a beautiful field covered with colorful flowers, and each of them radiated an extraordinary divine light. And the same light shone on Nastenka's chest. These two sources embraced each other and became even more divine and bright. And the whole world was filled with this light, the whole Universe, the whole Universe. And there was no grief or sorrow in this World. It simply forgot about it, as if they never existed at all. And everyone whom the little girl met on her way shone with the same light of love.

The conversation with her mother and this dream remained forever in the heart of little Nastenka as a guiding star showing the direction of the Way.

To love oneself is not to harm oneself, and through oneself not to harm others. To become light and to shine.

It's simple. From the word – very.

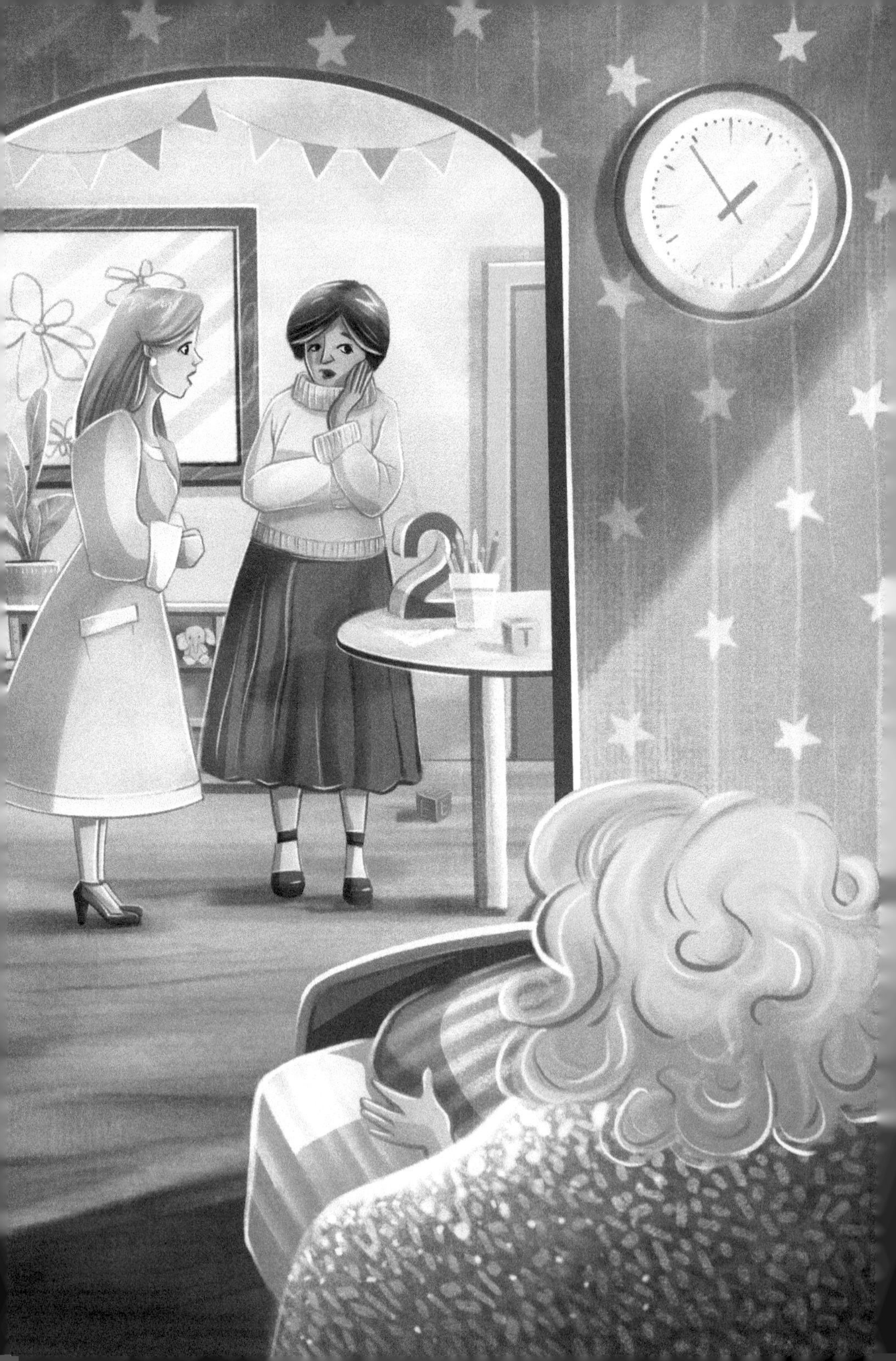

Chapter two

THE TEST OF HAPPINESS

– Mommy, why do people suffer?– Nastenka asked on the way home from kindergarten.

Mom looked at her daughter in surprise.

– Why are you suddenly interested in this?– she asked her daughter.

– I heard Tatyana Nikolayevna complaining to the nurse about her cursed life today.

Mom smiled slightly at Nastenka's words:

– Who says she has a cursed life?

– Tatyana Nikolayevna herself. She said: "I don't know what to do with this cursed life."

– What was that about? When did she say that?

– When all the children were asleep. She talked about how she was suffering alone. I couldn't sleep. I had all sorts of thoughts in my head.

– And what were those thoughts?

– That's why life can be cursed and why people get hurt. Why, Mom, is this happening?

– What else did Tatyana Nikolayevna say that made you so interested in this question?

– She said that man was created to suffer. So I thought about it. What, now I'll suffer too, and I'll have a cursed life?

Mom smiled:

– How do you want it to be?

– I don't want to suffer! I want to live happily!

– That's a good wish,– Mom said.– You see, people are different. And everyone's life is different. Some people suffer because
they can't get along with themselves. And if they can't get along
with themselves, life doesn't work out.

– What's it like to be okay with yourself?

– It means understanding who you are, what you live for, what
you want to accomplish.

– Strange question… I'm Nastenka, a girl, your daughter.

– That's right, that's the way it is,– Mom replied.– That is only
one side of you, which is on the surface. And there is also that
which is in the depths. Hiding from the consciousness of man. And
it is this mystery that he comes to unravel in this life.

– Does everyone solve these riddles?

– Unfortunately, not everyone and not always. That's why they
suffer. But those who have solved it become happy. That is why
there is a belief that a person comes to this world for suffering,
so that, thanks to these trials, he can realize who he really is, and
eventually find happiness in being himself.

Nastenka was silent for the rest of the journey. After supper
she hugged her parents, said good night and went to bed.

In the morning, as soon as the first ray of sunshine appeared
on the horizon, Nastenka climbed under her mother's blanket and
kissed her mother and announced:

– Mom, I know who I am. I'm happiness! Your happiness,
Dad's happiness, Grandma's happiness and my own happiness!

Mom laughed merrily.

– Sounds happy!– She hugged her daughter tightly.– My happiness!

– Yes, Mommy! I know a person can be for more than just
suffering. He can also be for happiness! And then he is not on the
path of suffering. He is on the path of happiness!

– How's that?– Mom asked in surprise.

– Well, he comes into this world already happy. He just doesn't know it yet. I had a dream today. A little angel came to visit me, a beautiful little angel! He hugged me and said: You are happiness! And your path is the path of happiness!- When I grow up, I will definitely tell everyone this.

– Did he explain to you what 'trial by happiness' means?

– Yes, he said that a person is born happy. But he can easily lose this happiness and forget about it, and then spend his whole life looking for it somewhere far away. And not know that he is this happiness. But as soon as he finds out that happiness has not gone anywhere, he immediately becomes happy. Right away!

– How wise your little angel is,– Mom said affectionately, clasping Nastenka to her breast.– Will you remember that you are happiness?

– Yes, Mommy! I will remember it for the rest of my life! And you are happiness too, remember that! Can you imagine, we already have two happinesses! And Daddy! And Grandma, that's happiness too! And we're already four such happinesses!

– Wow, that sounds like four happinesses!

– That's right! And when I tell everyone about it, there will be even more happiness!

Mom looked at her little happiness and rejoiced. And when she remembered her happiness, she was even happier.– Here, indeed, is the test of happiness! The main thing is to be able to get along with this happiness, and then the whole life will become happiness,– she thought.– And when life becomes happiness, to be able to hold this happiness, so as not to return to the cycle of suffering, deciding that this is life.

Such is the test of happiness!

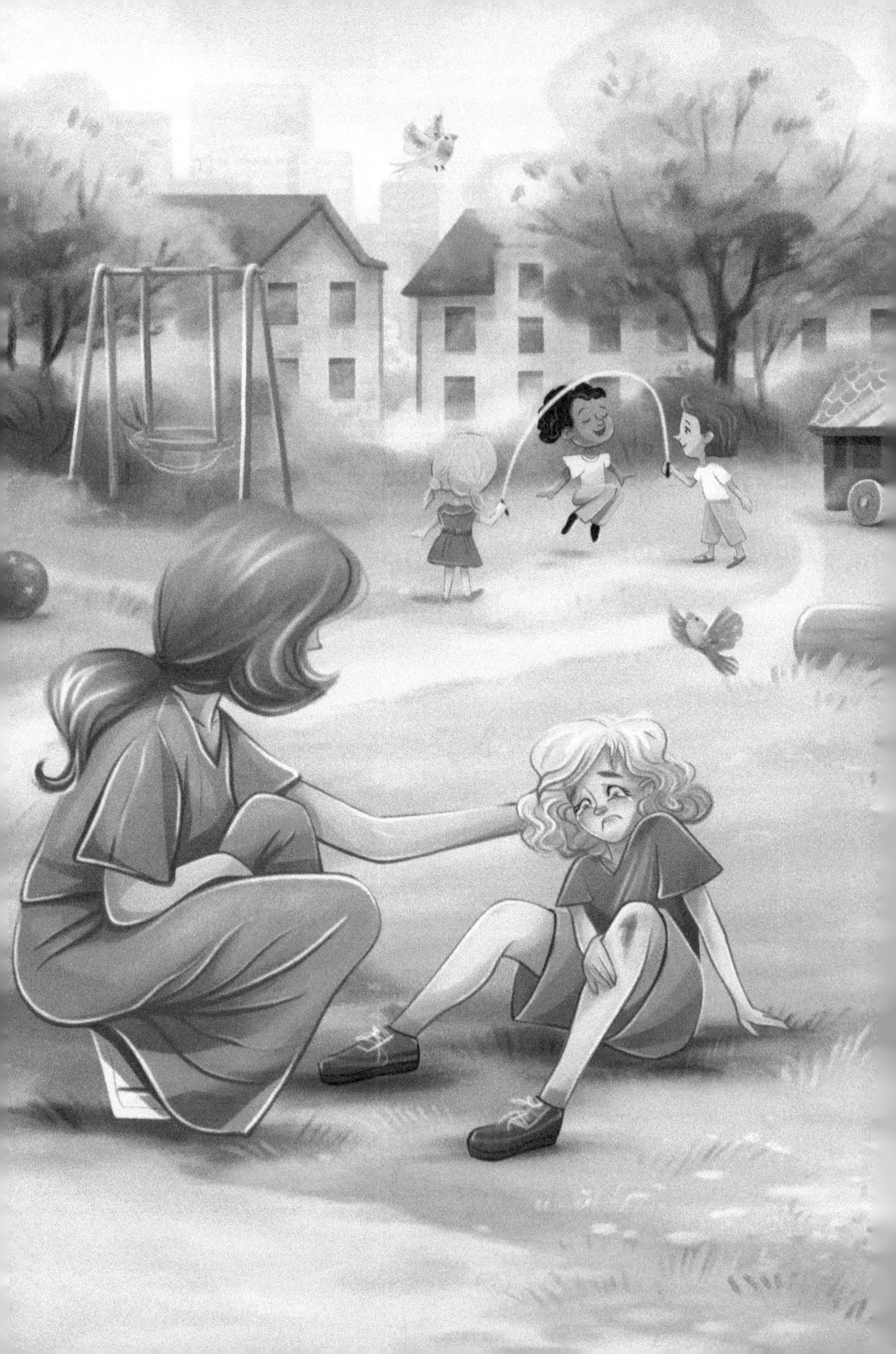

Chapter three

CAUSE AND EFFECT

  Nastenka was tearfully rubbing her knee to ease the pain of the fall. Her mother, seeing her daughter sitting on the pavement, came up and asked:

– What's wrong, my girl?

– I fell down,– Nastenka cried.

– Now, now, it's no big deal. Everyone falls down from time to time. I used to walk around with skinned knees when I was a kid, too,– her mother smiled and hugged Nastenka.

– Why did you fall?– Nastenka asked, wiping away her tears.

– What do you mean, why?– Mom was surprised by her daughter's question.

– I was running fast to get to the swings. I was afraid it would be occupied by other kids. So I tripped on a stone. Why'd you do that?

– That's how you are,– Mom smiled,– Always in a hurry to get somewhere.

– So, when you're in a hurry, you always fall down,– Nastenka concluded understandingly.

  Mom realized it was another moment to share a little wisdom with her daughter.

– You see, my girl, every action has a reason and there are consequences. Your desire to take a swing and not let the other kids get ahead of you started the process of rushing. Haste tends to lead to inattention. Inattention leads to unpleasant consequences. In your case, it led to a fall and a slight injury to your knee.

– So I started the process myself?– Nastenka said thoughtfully.

– Yes, my dear,– the mother took her daughter in her arms and sat down with her on the bench.– Our desires are the causes, and what they lead to is the consequence of those desires. But not only our desires. After all, in the beginning an idea is born, a thought, which awakens this desire or intention to do something, to say something. Only a person does not always think about what the realization of this intention or desire can lead to.

– That's right, Mommy,– I didn't think about the fact that my desire might make me fall. My thoughts were controlling my feet, which were running fast and didn't notice this rock that was in the way of my goal.

Mom laughed.

– How interesting, turns out it's your desire that's to blame for your fall?

– Who else?– Nastenka was genuinely surprised.– That's exactly what it is!

– How will you deal with your desires now?– Mom asked.

– I'm not going to listen to them,– Nastenka said as if she were cut off.

– Having desires is a good thing,– Mom said, gently stroking her daughter's head.– Without desires, mankind would not have achieved anything. It is natural to want something. But in order to achieve any goal, it is important to understand, firstly, why you need it, and, secondly, how to act to get the desired thing in the best way. And, most importantly, to realize that you are the reason for everything that happens to you.

– How's that?– Nastenka looked at her mom with wide-open eyes.

– Let's look at your example,– Mom suggested.– I'll try to make my assumptions, and you can correct me if I'm wrong.

– Come on,– Nastenka readily agreed.

– You saw a swing and you wanted to ride it, right?

Nastenka nodded her head silently.

– You saw some kids near the swings and assumed that they would want to ride too, and you would have to wait a long time. Or, alternatively, you wanted to be the first one to take the swing. What really happened?

– To be honest, Mom, I wanted to be the first one to take that swing,– Nastenka admitted.

– Well, now I suggest we figure out how important was it to be the first to take the swings? What could have gone wrong if someone else had taken them first?

Nastenka thought for a moment. It was obvious that the process of reflection was serious, all the pros and cons were being weighed. Her mother did not hurry her daughter.

– You know, Mom, I get it,– Nastenka said slowly.– By and large, it wasn't that important to be first on that swing. After all, I had just gone out for a walk, and I had plenty of time to walk. Then none of the guys looked in the direction of the swings, they were playing some game and were engrossed in it. And it was safe for me to walk to that swing and ride as long as I wanted. And even if someone took the swing first, it wouldn't be a big deal. I could ask him to let me ride on it too.

– You are so clever, my daughter,– her mother hugged Nastenka.– You see, when you can see the whole picture, it is easier for you to understand how to do the best thing. And then your wish comes true, and your knees, let's say, stay intact!

– Now I know how to act!– getting off her mother's lap, Nastenka said.– I realized that desires are born in me, so I am the mistress of these desires. And then it is important for me to understand whether this desire is so necessary to fulfill, or if it can be changed to make me feel better. And when I realize that it is this desire that I want to fulfill, then I will think how I can do it better. And I certainly know now that there is no need to hurry.

– That's right, my girl! There's no need for haste in life. It is true that sometimes you have to act quickly, but it has nothing to do with haste. And we'll definitely talk about it sometime, too.

– Okay, Mommy,– Nastenka hugged her mother and ran to the playground. But now she looked under her feet and chose a road without bumps and rocks, sometimes stopping and looking around, as if she wanted to see the whole picture, to explore all the space around her, so that next time reaching the goal would be easy and pleasant.

After all, the consequence can be not only painful, but also very pleasant. Now Nastenka knew that for sure!

Wise tales for children and adults

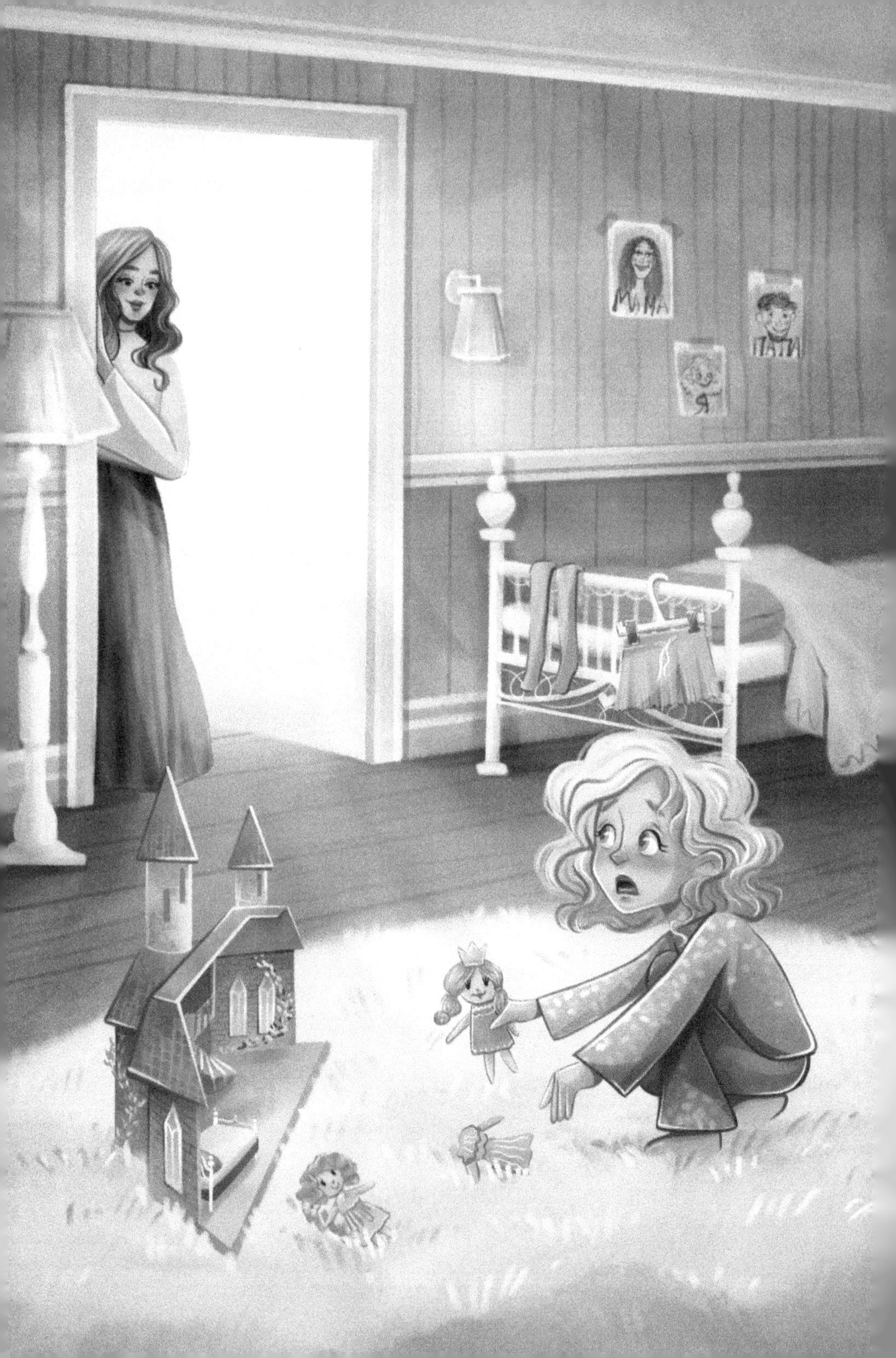
МАМА
ПАПА
Я

Chapter four

QUICKLY, BUT NOT IN A HURRY

– Mommy, what does it mean when people say "quickly, but not in a hurry"?– Nastenka asked, sitting down on the sofa next to her mother.– You promised to tell me.

Mom gave her a hug and said:

– Well, let's speculate.

– Okay,– agreed Nastenka.

– Think about it and answer me this question: when you are in a hurry to get somewhere, do you get everything done?

Nastenka thought for a moment.

– Well, when I play too much before I go to daycare, I can barely get my tights on right, and even then the heel can be out of place, and it's very uncomfortable to walk. And I get mad.

– How do you feel when you're in a hurry to put on your tights?

– I worry that I'm late and I'm making you late and I feel like crying because I can't deal with it.

Mom kissed Nastenka and said:

– My girl, thank you for sharing your experiences with me. It's very important to me. Now let's look at this situation. When you realize that you are playing and you don't have much time, you probably get scared that you won't have time and make rash movements, because all your attention is focused on your experience and not on the actions themselves, right?

– Yes, Mommy, I am very anxious and my arms won't listen to me and my legs don't want to get dressed!

– What an interesting story you tell about yourself! It turns out that your mind, your experiences– they are also called emotions– and your body are acting uncoordinated, like the swan, the crayfish and the pike in the famous fable by I.A. Krylov. Do you remember when we read it?

– I remember! – Nastenka cheered up.

– So, – my mother continued,–it turns out that a person whose head, body and emotions live on their own is often in a state of hurry and is unable to perform actions that could lead him to the desired result. In your case, getting your tights on correctly. That's how haste works. Get it?

– Yes, – Nastenka sighed, – I've learned. And what should I do now? I can play games again, can't I?

– You can if you don't direct your attention to the task that's important to accomplish first.

– Oh, Mommy, I got it! – Nastenka jumped. – I got it! I have to get dressed first, and then play!

Mom laughed.

– That's a great solution! That is, you first perform those actions that are most important, and then do what you want to do, do I understand you correctly?

– Yes! – and suddenly Nastenka got sad. – What if I forget to get dressed first again? What if I want to play first again and I play, what should I do then, mom?

Mom smiled.

– Everything happens in life,– she reassured Nastenka.– The

most important thing is not to give in to your emotions. Don't let them control you. Otherwise, the swan, the crayfish and the pike will start their work again. And for such a case there is a magic word that can help you.

– A magic word?– Nastenka wondered.

– Yes, the magic word. And it's STOP.

– STOP?!

– Yeah, STOP. Let's play. Imagine that it's morning and you have to get ready for kindergarten, and you decide to play for a minute with your favorite doll and get lost. Bring her over here.

Nastenka ran to her room and brought out her toy friend with her entire closet.

– I'll change her,– Nastenka sat down in the middle of the room and started picking out a new costume for her toy.

– And when I say to you,– Nastenka, we're coming out– You do everything as you usually do when you're in a hurry, but only after you hear my words, say to yourself STOP. Okay?

– Okay, Mommy,– Nastenka replied, becoming more and more immersed in the game.

Mom held out for a while, letting her daughter get as engrossed in what was happening as possible, and then she said loudly:

– Nastenka, we're coming out!

Nastenka froze for a second, looked in horror at the doll dresses scattered on the floor, jumped up and.... screamed:

– STOP!!!

She stood silently for a few seconds, and then with measured movements she quickly gathered up all the toys and ran to her room. Two minutes later she was standing in her tights, happy and joyful.

– What's wrong with you?– Mom asked, smiling.

– Mommy, look how great my tights fit! My hands finally agreed with my feet! My hands took their time and my legs didn't fight back!

– Congratulations, my dear! How did you feel when you heard my voice?

– At first I was afraid that I wouldn't make it again, but then I remembered the magic word, and it was as if it had driven my fear out of me and showed me how to act. Remember when we went camping, my dad had a map with all the stops, turns, and dangerous places marked on it? Well, it was like I had that map in my head. And then I got through everything quickly. I had no worries or anxiety because I knew what to do after what. How great it is, mommy, when you have such a map in your head!– Nastenka ran up to her mom and hugged her.

Mom stroked Nastenka's head and pronounced:

– There, now you know the difference between being fast and being in a hurry.

– Yes! When I'm in a hurry, I get nervous, and when I do fast, I have a map in my head. And the magic word STOP that turns hurry into fast!

Nastenka and her mom played the magic game STOP for a long time. Her daughter learned to build maps in her head, and her mom helped her to cope with her emotions. And one more lesson Nastenka learned that day was to do important things first, so that later there would be time to do her favorite things and get maximum pleasure from it.

That's the story!

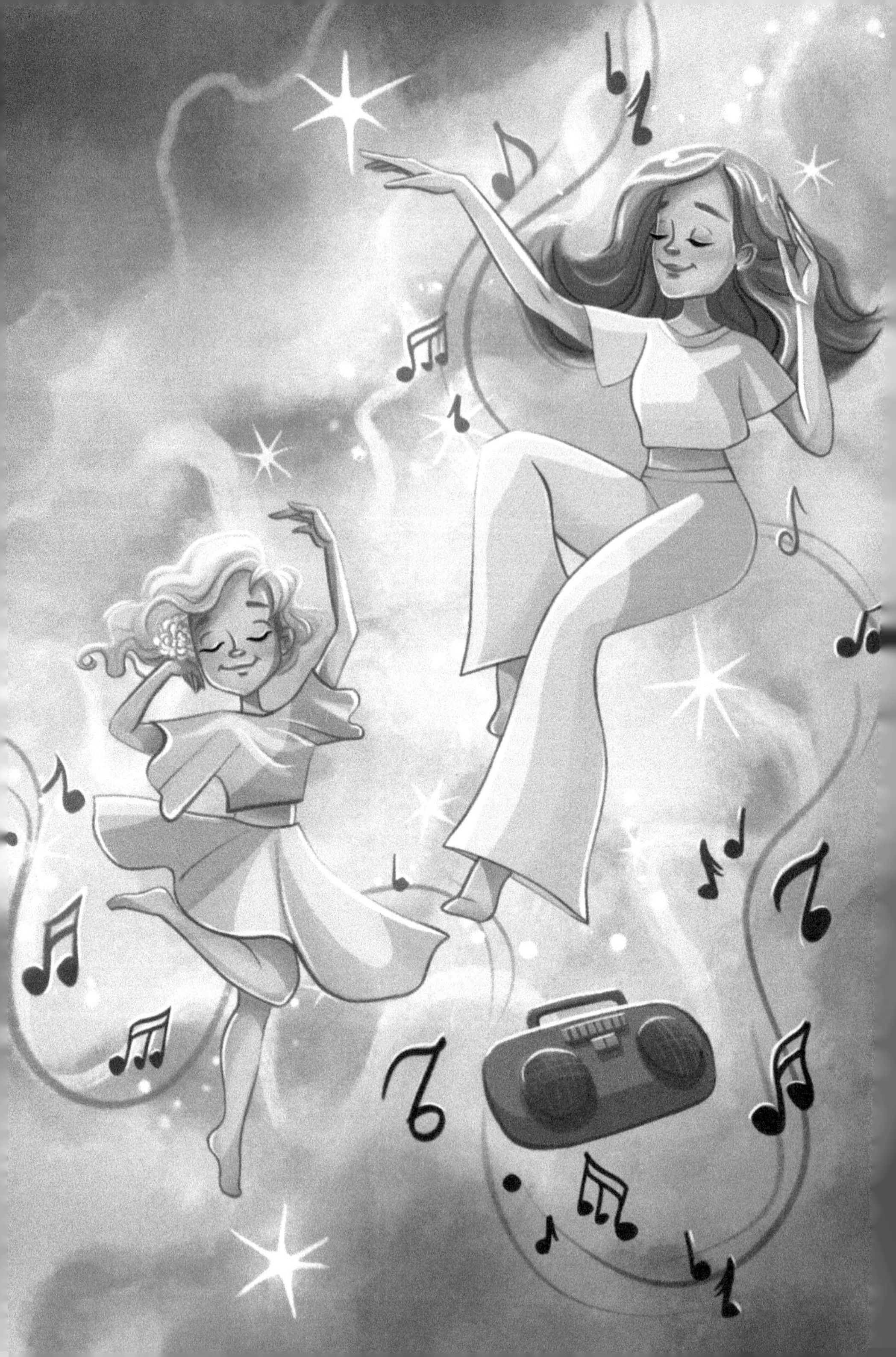

Chapter five

ON THE SAME WAVELENGTH

– Mom, what does it mean to be on the same wavelength?– Nastenka asked, buttoning up her coat.

– Did you overhear someone else's conversation again today?– Mom smiled.

– It wasn't my fault that the ladies were talking loudly,– Nastenka frowned.– And my ears are just good at hearing.

– You are my idea catcher!– Mom laughed and hugged her daughter.– You know, it's great that your ears are attuned to life's important questions. That way, I can share my wisdom with you and you can learn different ways to solve life's problems.

– Then my ears are wise too!– Nastenka said proudly.

– Yes, very much!– Mom confirmed.– The main thing is that they should remain so wise as not to get involved in other people's conversation when it is meant only for those who are speaking.

– I understand, Mommy,– Nastenka nodded eagerly.– They are not nosy.

Her mother stroked her daughter's head affectionately, and they walked home together, holding hands. On the way, her mother shared an interesting story with Nastenka.

– Imagine you are listening to the radio. You usually choose the channel that plays children's songs or tells stories. Sometimes we listen to it together. At that moment, we are close, we are tuned in to the same stories, we are both interested. We have the same interest in what's going on. And most importantly, we like it. That's what it means to be on the same wavelength– to feel the same way, to think the same way, to show interest in the same things. But sometimes it's more important for me to listen to something else.

Do you think I or you can hear the channel where I usually listen to audiobooks if the radio is tuned in to the children's channel?

– Of course not,– Nastenka looked at her mother in surprise.– How can we hear it if we have to switch the radio to hear it?

– That's right,– Mom nodded.– Now you understand that there are different waves, and to hear one wave it is important to switch to it from another?

– Yes, I understand,– said Nastenka.

– Do you want me to tell you why some people only see the bad and others only see the good?

– Yes, Mommy, I do!– Nastenka got excited.

– Then listen. Man, too, has his own wave. He himself is that wave. Each wave has its own feelings, its own emotions, its own thoughts, its own power, its own energy. And he, like a radio, transmits all this to the surrounding space. When a person thinks about bad things, gets angry, resentful, anxious, he creates a wave of anger, resentment, anxiety. And until he switches to another wave, he will not be able to rejoice, enjoy life, laugh, feel pleasure. It's just not available to him. There are no such programs on his channel.

But if he looks at the world with a smile, he has peace inside, his eyes are attuned to beauty and his ears to kindness, then his channel will radiate these states, and he himself will pick them up from the world around him.

– So that's why some people are always complaining and others are always happy?– Nastenka guessed.

– That's right, my dear!– Mom said affectionately.– There was a scientist named Albert Einstein. He studied nature and the laws by which it exists. So, he said that the waves sent by us connect with the same waves and return to us amplified. So if you want to receive more love, learn how to send love yourself.

– Yes, yes, Mommy, I remember you telling me what it means to love yourself. I understand it even more now. People who are angry, swearing, resentful, they are on the same wavelength with the same people. And their anger, their resentment is even more amplified. And those who rejoice are on the same wavelength with those who also rejoice. And they have a lot of joy! And I choose the wave of joy!

– I agree with you, my girl! We'll be with you on a wave of joy!– smiled Mom.

– Oh, Mommy, what if I get on the wave of sadness, what should I do then?– Nastenka got worried.

– Don't worry, dear,– her mother reassured her.– Anyone can be sad. But if you are used to living on a wave of joy, your sadness will not last long, and you will soon want to switch to your own wave. The main thing is to decide where you want to be– at the bottom or at the top.

– I've decided, Mommy, I'm going to learn to live on a wave of joy, allow myself to be sad sometimes, but then switch back to my wave. Oh, how exciting! Let's play! I'll pretend to be sad, and then I'll switch and be happy!

– Come on,– the mother encouraged her daughter.– Then I suggest that you think of a joy switch. When you do, it will be easier for you to get back on your wavelength.

– Oh, Mommy, what a great idea! This is going to be our radio knob. It's easy for me to twist it to change it to my favorite channel.

– It's a deal,– Mom said as she opened the door to the house.

All evening Nastenka and her mother played a new game, which they called "On the Wave of Joy". They were on the same wavelength and it gave them great pleasure.

Now you too can play this game with your loved ones. And you too will learn to live in a state of joy, so that you can always be on the same wavelength with those who have also chosen to live in joy!

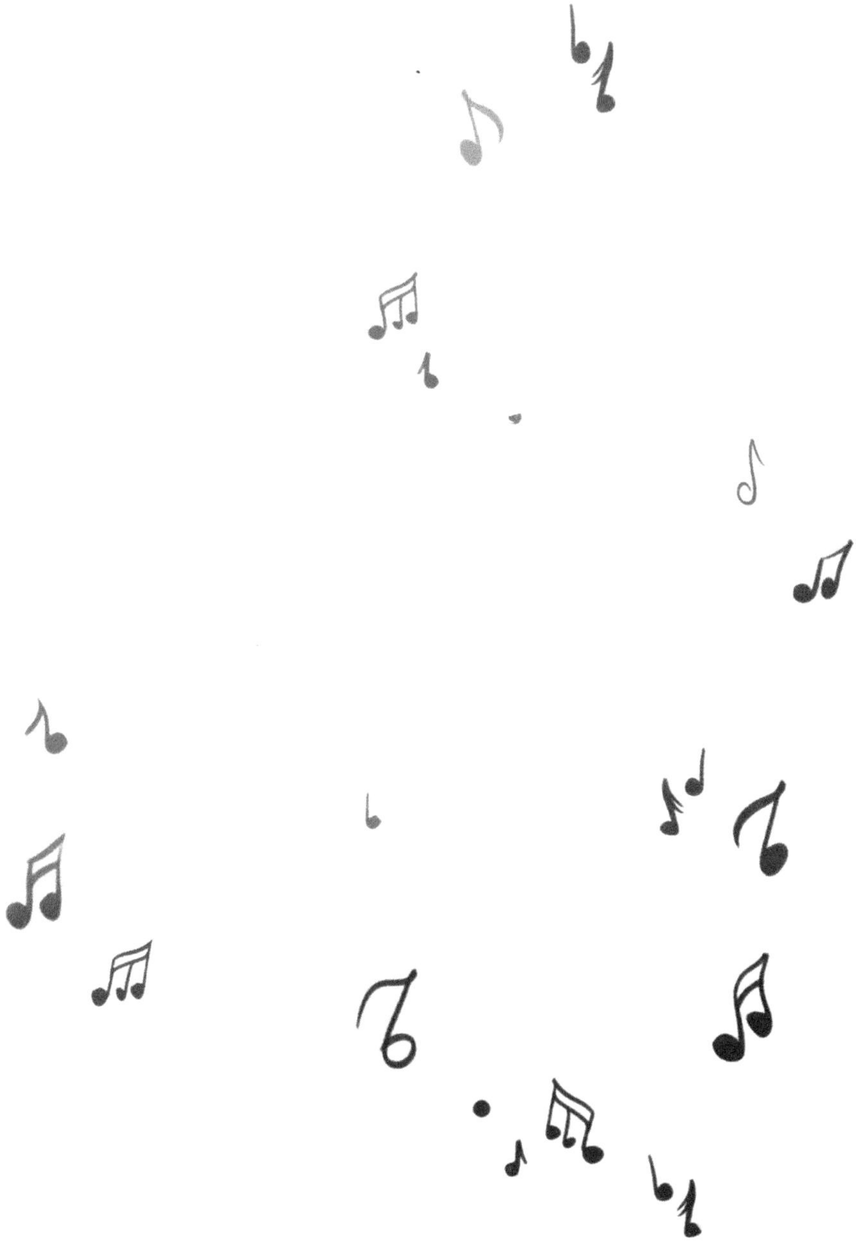

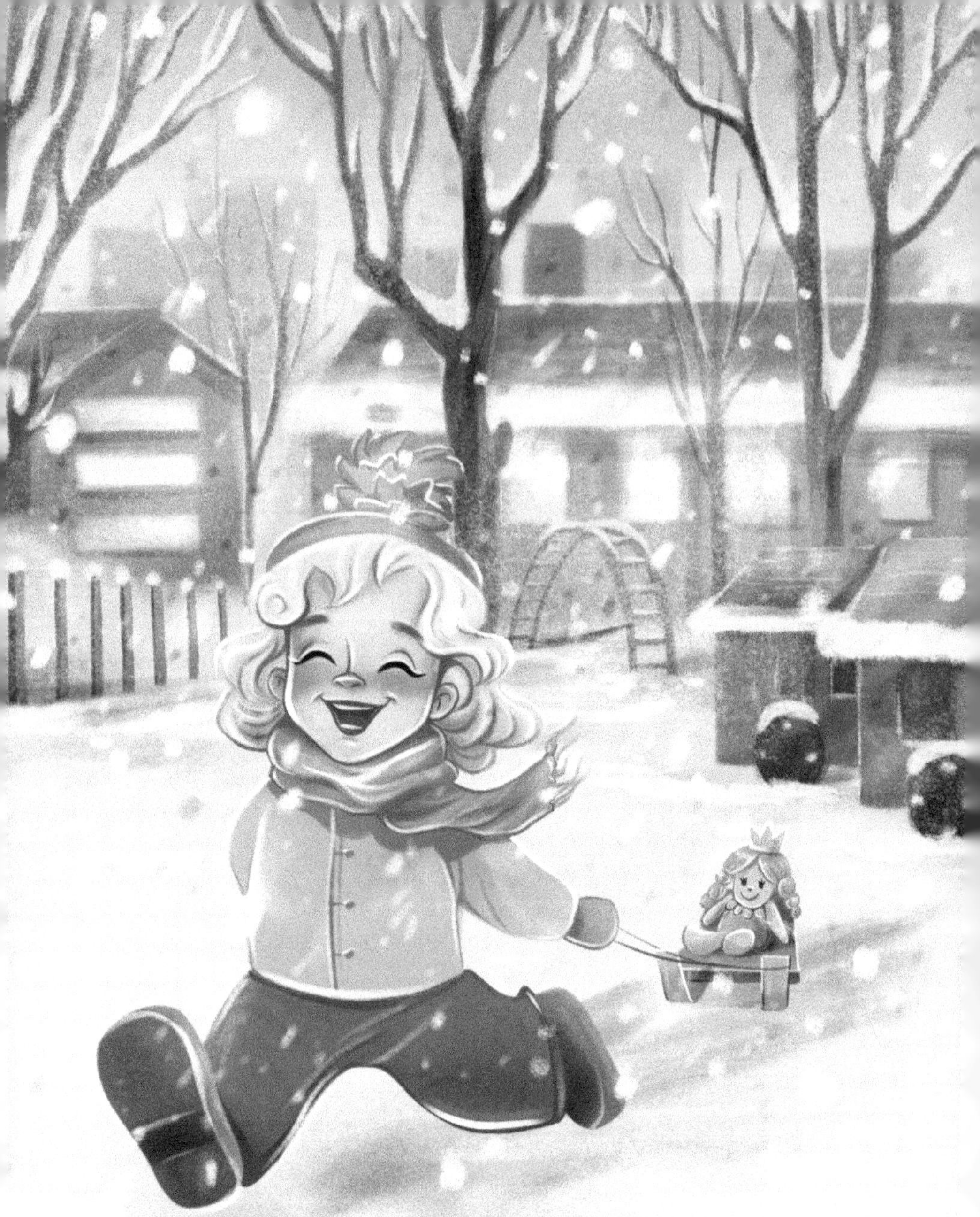

Chapter six

THERE'S ALWAYS
A WAY OUT

– Well, there's a snowstorm outside, and now we can't go anywhere,– Nastenka said, looking out the window.– And I was so looking forward to sledding today! Mommy, why is it always like this?

– What's always like this?– Mom asked, smiling.

– As soon as you think of something, plan something, something is bound to go wrong!

– Who told you that?

– I decided it myself. I've already broken my plans twice,– Nastenka said indignantly.

– And you decided that if something happened twice, it will always be like that?– watching her daughter's reaction, her mother smiled.

– Oh!– Nastenka exclaimed.– I guess so.

– And you're the one who wants your plans to go awry?– Mom decided to tease her daughter a little.

– No, of course not! I want them to be realized!– Nastenka answered decisively.– But I just don't know how to do it. Can you help me, Mom?

– I'd love to!– answered the mother and offered to make herself comfortable on the sofa.– I'm going to tell you a terrible secret,– Mom said mysteriously.– There is always a way out. And there is always a solution. It's just that you may not see and realize all the options at once. And in order to see and realize them, you need to calm down and think. Do you remember when we practiced the magic word STOP?

– Yes, Mommy, I remember, – Nastenka answered, still not quite understanding what her mother was saying.

– So here goes. In any situation, when setting any goal, it is important to consider at least three variants of possible developments. The first is that everything will happen very, very well, exactly as planned, and even better. The second – it will happen, but it will not give much pleasure, or everything will remain as it is. And the third – it will be worse than you expected. In these three situations, we will experience different emotions. Think about it, how will you feel in the first case?

– Joy and happiness, – Nastenka smiled.

– And the second one?

– Probably nothing special, – Nastenka thought to herself.

– And the third?

– I'll be upset, – the daughter replied with a frown.

– Do you know what the reason for this is?– Mom asked, further intriguing her daughter.

– Which one? – Nastenka looked carefully into her mother's eyes.

– Because a person is attached to the situation, the result and does not consider other options for achieving the conceived goal. In fact, there can be a lot of options for the development of events. You already know three. There is a fourth, but you don't see it, and no one knows the fifth.

– Wow, how interesting,– Nastenka said excitedly.– And what to do?

— It is important to understand why you are setting this or that goal, what exactly you want to achieve. And, based on that, consider ways to achieve it. You wanted to go sledding, right?

— Yes, Mommy!— answered Nastenka.

— And for what purpose?

— What do you mean?— Nastenka asked in surprise.

— What did you want to get out of this ride?

— Take a walk, enjoy the snow, breathe in the fresh winter air....

— But you were bothered by the weather, right?

— Yeah.

— What exactly made you uncomfortable? The blizzard?

— Yeah.

— Can't you go sledding in a snowstorm, breathe fresh air, enjoy the snow?

— You can, I guess...— Nastenka looked at her mother in surprise.

— Of course you can!— laughed Mom.— It's just important to dress appropriately and not to go long distances! After all, you can go sledding in the yard, moving downwind. Moving against the wind, changing position on the sled. And to stay warm....

— Not only to sit in the sled, but also to roll them!— picked up Nastenka.

— That's right, my girl!— Mom supported her daughter.— You see how many solutions we have found at once!

— Yay! I'm going out! And my dream will come true!— Nastenka jumped with joy and ran to get dressed.

Mom lovingly watched as Nastenka implemented conscious decisions, taking great pleasure in it.

The walk was a success. Nastenka not only rode on the sleds, but also drove them herself, putting her favorite doll as a passenger.

She also enjoyed playing snowballs with her parents. And together with them she drew angels in the snow, falling on her back in the snowdrift and waving her arms as if they were wings. She had seen this in one of the movies.

She came home happy. She realized her dream– a set of desires hidden in the phrase 'sledding'. Warm clothes and movement kept her from freezing. She didn't think about playing snowballs– the idea came later. And the picture on the wall of the house told her about the angels. That's how the fourth and fifth versions of events became reality.

And now Nastenka knew that there was always a way out and a solution. It is just important to think a little and let yourself find the solution. And also to let something happen that you don't know about and that no one knows about.

Just let it happen!

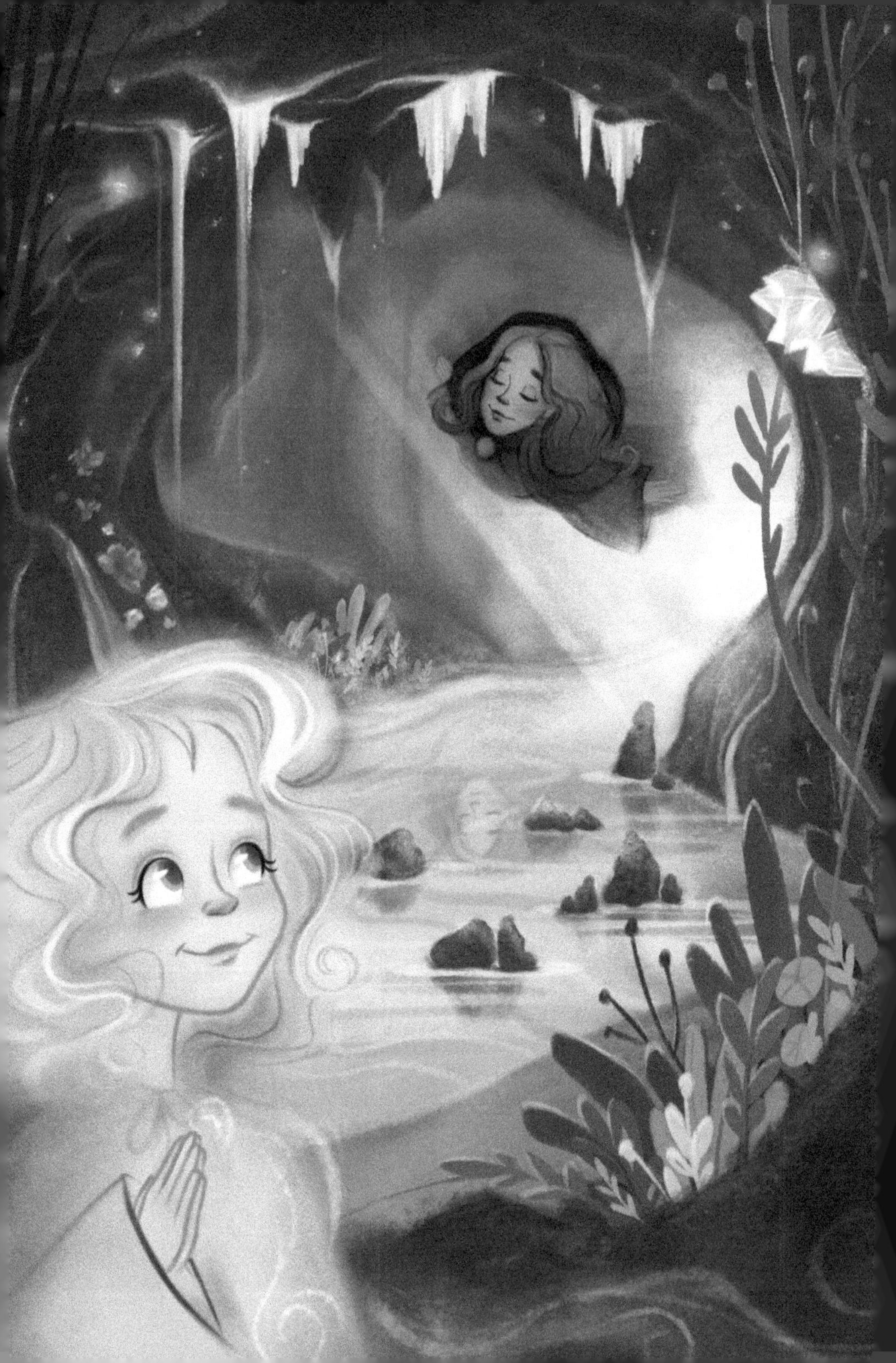

Chapter seven

BREEZE

– Mommy, tell me a story,– Nastenka asked, diving into bed.

– What kind of story do you want?– Mom smiled.

– An interesting one.

– An interesting one?– Mom laughed.– Well, make yourself comfortable, and I'll tell you a story about the breeze.

– Oh, how interesting!– Nastenka wrapped herself in a blanket and prepared to listen attentively.

Mom sat down on Nastenka's bed and began the story.

– Once upon a time, there was a boy. He loved to explore. One day he was running through the forest and met an unusual old man. The old man was dressed in white clothes, holding a staff in his hands, and it was obvious that he had traveled a long way.

The boy said hello to him and offered him the water he had in the vessel he usually took with him on his walks. The old man thanked him and sat down on a rock near the road. After drinking the water, he returned the vessel to the boy and asked:

– How did you end up in this forest? Aren't you afraid to be alone, because there are many animals here?

– No, I'm not scared at all, I love walking in the forest,– the boy answered,– there are so many unusual things to see here! Today I met you. And surely you have an interesting story to share while you are resting.

The old man smiled:

– Yes, I have many stories, as I have lived a long and complicated life. Well, then, listen up.

When I was young, I went to an elder from whom I wanted to learn the wisdom of life. And during one of his lessons he told me this story. In far, far away times there lived a little Wind. He lived among high mountains and loved to play, flying over the mountain ranges and enjoying their majesty and his courage, because he rose so high, sometimes flying into the clouds, resting on the highest peak.

And he liked to stir and disperse them. And sometimes he would calm down and rest on the soft surface of those cloud caps.

And then one day he decided to see what was below. After all, he had never been there before. And the Wind began to descend lower and lower until he came to a deep gorge. This gorge was incredibly beautiful and stretched for hundreds and hundreds of kilometers. There were many caves in it, which were a complex labyrinth. And it so happened that Wind got lost in it.

And in this gorge lived the Spirit, who guarded this gorge. And he did not like his peace to be disturbed by anyone, and especially did not like those who considered themselves stronger than him. And few people would get out of the gorge if they awakened the Spirit and challenged him.

One day, a small dwarf who thought he was stronger than all the mountains put together wanted to become the master of this gorge. So the Spirit put him in chains and hid him in the deepest cave.

Wind wandered through the maze for a long time until he found himself in the very cave in which the little dwarf had been chained.

How excited the little dwarf was when he saw Wind.

– Greetings, Wind!– exclaimed the dwarf.– What are you doing here?

– I'm lost,– said the Windy Man sadly,– and I don't know how to get out of here. I have never flown below. My friends have always been mountain tops and clouds.

– How did you get here?– The dwarf inquired.

– I just wanted to see new lands, because I love learning new things so much.

– Well, if you take these chains off me, I'll get you out of here,– the little dwarf smiled slyly.

– Who chained you?– Wind asked.

– The evil spirit that rules this whole gorge. He doesn't like guests and always treats them that way.

The breeze thought for a moment. As he flew through the gorge and its caves, no one had met him, much less wanted to put him in chains.

– The spirit is very cunning,– continued the little dwarf in an in-gratiating voice. He never helps anyone to get out of the labyrinth of his gorge. And if you don't help me, you will die. Only I can help you.

Wind was very kind, his parents always taught him to help the weak.

– If you help me, you will be able to fly freely over the tops of the mountains, and through this and other gorges, and there will be no danger. And together we can destroy this labyrinth so that no one else will ever get into a situation like you and me.

The little dwarf's plan was very cunning. With Wind's help, he wanted to divert the Gorge Spirit's attention and, by sacrificing Wind, seize power in this mountain range.

Wind was confused. On the one hand he wanted to help the little dwarf, but on the other hand he did not want to participate in the destruction of the gorge. After all, it was so beautiful. And each cave also held some secrets and riddles that Wind wanted to solve.

And he had never seen the Spirit of the Cave and had never met him, so he did not know if the little dwarf was telling the truth. But the little dwarf was very cunning. He almost succeeded in persuading the Wind to conspire with him and carry out his devious plan. And he agreed, believing the false words of the little dwarf. All the more he saw no other way out.

But the Wind was able to tear off only one chain out of ten that held the little dwarf in the cave, because he had been wandering through the labyrinth of caves for a very long time and was very tired, and the chains were heavy and strong.

– Let me get some rest, – Wind asked the little dwarf. – In the morning I will be strong enough to help you take off the rest of the chains. And so it was agreed.

The little dwarf was left with his thoughts on how to overthrow and destroy the Gorge Spirit and the Wind, and the Wind fell into a deep sleep, remembering his grandmother's saying–the morning is wiser than the evening-.

At night, Wind had a wonderful dream. The Spirit of the Gorge came to him and said:

– I'm glad to welcome you, Wind. It is the first time you have come down from the top of the mountains into my gorge and have become acquainted with the labyrinth of caves. I did not disturb you or try to help you, because I did not want to disturb your journey. There is much to see and learn here.

After all, you can only share your own experiences. And unless you learn how to find your way out of every cave in my gorge, you will never gain the power of wisdom and be able to teach it to your brothers and sisters and pass it on to your children. For this reason alone, I have not interfered with the course of events.

Remember, I will never harm anyone who carefully tends to my domain. And you can always turn to me when you lose hope.

In the morning, Wind woke up with the realization that he didn't know the whole situation. And, speaking only to the little dwarf, he had jumped to conclusions. He flew out of the cave where the little dwarf was dozing and went in search of the Gorge Spirit.

The spirit of the gorge did not wait long. He welcomed his guest with joy and showed him all the beauties around him. And the Spirit told Wind a little secret about how to get out of the most confusing cave in his gorge.

– You can always call out to me. And I will come to you exactly at the moment when you are calm and ready to hear me. And for this purpose it is important for you to train your mind to be quiet.

And when your mind is trained to silence and you can hear me, you will always find a way out of the most confusing cave, because you will have knowledge.

In each cave you will be met by a little dwarf who will tell you the easiest but wrong decision. And only you can make the choice to hear me or listen to him. And when you learn to keep your mind in silence and hear me, you will have an opportunity to feel your inner power and realize your greatness. For with the help of your blowing anyone can find a way out of the cave.

And from then on the Wind was no longer afraid to go down into the gorge and fly in the most confusing caves, because he could hear the Spirit of the gorge and listen to himself. Soon he passed on all his knowledge to his brothers and sisters, and after a while to his children. His knowledge of the labyrinth of the gorge helped explorers and hikers find the right path. I don't know what happened to that Wind. He probably lives in this gorge now, passing on his experience to all who come to learn his wisdom and make friends with the Spirit of the gorge.

The old man was silent, and the boy realized that while he was listening to the story, too much time had passed and he might be lost. He thanked the old man and jumped out of the forest, forgetting both the old man and his story on the way. Only the pleasant memory of something interesting and very important that he had learned today warmed his heart, filling him with joy and happiness.

The sun was setting behind the horizon, and its last rays were gently saying goodbye to the tops of the trees. The world was sinking into silence, the breath of the earth was calming down, and everything around acquired harmony, filling every grain of existence with love...

Mom looked at Nastenka. She was sniffling quietly, hugging the edge of the blanket, smiling in her sleep. Apparently, she was also gaining some wisdom, having met her Gorge Spirit. Her mother kissed her daughter softly on the forehead and left the room, closing the door behind her. She did not want to disturb her daughter from traveling through the labyrinths of her caves under the guidance of her inner mentor, whom it was important to be able to hear. And when a person hears the voice of his Mentor, he always chooses the right path.

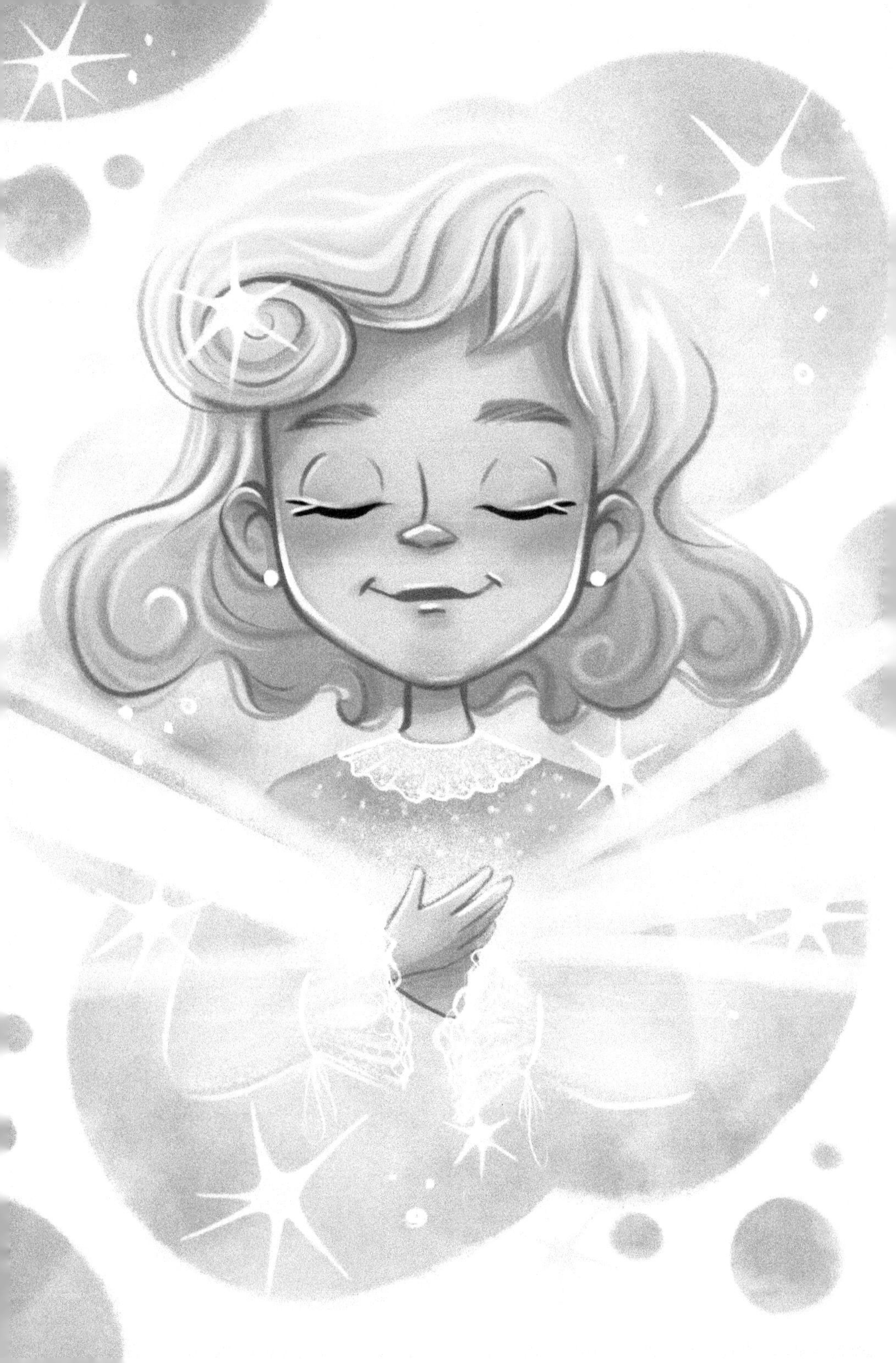

Chapter eight

HAPPINESS TO BE YOURSELF

– How was your day?– asked Nastenka's mother, picking her up from kindergarten.

– Good, Mommy,– Nastenka replied cheerfully.– So good that I have a whole bunch of questions for you!

– A whole bunch of them?– Mom laughed.

– Yes, and these are very important questions for me,– Nastenka said seriously.

– Well, if they are so important,– Mom also became serious to support her daughter,– then I will try to answer them for you. I suggest you get ready and go for a walk, it's a beautiful warm evening, and we'll philosophize at home. You'll gather your thoughts, and I'll prepare for a serious conversation. How's that?

– Okay, Mammy,– Nastenka nodded, getting ready to go home.

It was indeed a marvelous evening. The wind had died down, and only occasionally the treetops rustled, as if sharing the day's adventures and news. The air was fresh and clean. Filled with the aromas of club petunias, he shared them with passersby strolling along the park alleys. Nastenka chirped merrily, admiring the blossoming magnolia and the beauty of the blossoming apple trees.

After dinner, climbing up on her favorite couch and sitting down next to her mother, she said:

– So, shall we talk?

Mom laughed, hugged her daughter gently and said:

– Let's talk.

– Mom, today I was called a black sheep. At first I was offended, but then I remembered that you could help me figure it out, so I calmed down.

– And who gave you that name?

– Tatyana Nikolayevna.

– Why did she call you that?

– Today we talked about who dreams of becoming what when they grow up. Almost everyone said they wanted to earn a lot and become rich. And I said that I wanted to be useful to the world.

– How do you want to be useful to the world?– Mom asked.

– I want people on earth to be happy. Like me.

– How do you want it to happen?

– I don't know yet. But I know for sure that my happiness can help others to become happy too! And I also know that you have a story that is very wise, and you will tell it to me today!

– And what's the story behind that?– Mom smiled.

– About the white crow. Why are people called that when they think differently from everyone else? Why is it hard to be a white crow? Why aren't they loved? Why, Mom?

– What makes you think white crows aren't loved?

– Tatyana Nikolayevna. She said it would be difficult for me in life.

– And you believed it?

– A little bit. I was confused.

– Well, today I'm going to tell you a story. It's about a white squirrel. I think you will find answers to your questions in it,– said Mommy,– and decide whether it is hard to be a squirrel or not.

54

– Okay, Mommy, I'm ready,– Nastenka hugged the small pillow and prepared to listen.

– In long, long ago times,– the mother began,– there lived a squirrel. It was different from its fellows in that it was completely white. It was also the most agile, shrewd and hardy squirrel in its pack.

And then came the hard times. In the forests where the squirrel flock lived, there came severe frosts, which had not been seen in these places for two or three hundred years. Many squirrels in neighboring forests could not withstand such cold and died. And only the white squirrel dared to come out of the hollow in these fierce frosts and bring the prey, which it had saved in the whole forest during the summer.

Thanks to this squirrel's foresight and resourcefulness, her relatives survived because she brought them food directly to the hollow tree and supported them in their hour of need. And the squirrels treated her with great respect and appreciated her kindness and wisdom.

But still the white squirrel was unhappy.– Why was I born so white and lonely? Why am I not like everyone else? I can never be happy and have a family,– she often said to herself, sitting alone in her hollow tree.

The white squirrel suffered for a long time, and one day she decided to go to distant forests in the hope of finding similar squirrels. She hoped at least there to meet her chosen one. But before she set off, she decided to talk to a wise old squirrel who lived at the edge of the forest in the hollow of an ancient oak tree.

– Why do you want to leave? After all, all our squirrels love and respect you,– asked the wise squirrel.

– Who would want to have children with an albino squirrel?–

replied the white squirrel sadly.– I dream of having children and becoming a mother!

– Why do you need a family and children?– the old squirrel asked.

– Looking at my children, I will feel like the happiest squirrel in the world! They will be agile and strong. And I will be proud that I gave them this life and was able to pass on my wisdom.

– You don't need to run away to distant forests for that. Anyone would be happy to be your chosen one. After all, you saved the life of me and all our squirrels. You will bring wonderful offspring that will also be hardy. And all our generations will become wiser, stronger and more resilient,– said the wise squirrel.

The white squirrel thought about the words of the wise old squirrel and thanked her and ran away. She raced swiftly through the snow-covered forest, and her heart filled with joy and her head resounded,– You will bring wonderful offspring who will also be hardy... all our generations will become wiser, stronger, and more resilient...– And as she hopped from branch to branch, the white squirrel realized her worth, her Mission. And on her way she met a male squirrel who did not dare to offer the albino squirrel his hand and heart for a long time. He was afraid that she would refuse him.

And for the next part of the journey they traveled together.

Years passed. The pack of red and white squirrels grew. They were resilient, wise, hardy. They easily survived in the harshest conditions. Thanks to their special skills, they learned to revive forests, carrying fruits and seeds, which, once in the ground, sprouted new trees. And the forest became thicker and cozier. And other packs came and inhabited the forest, learning wisdom from the red and white pack.

The white squirrel lived a long and happy life. Only once did she remember her suffering. It was the day she told her grandchildren how extraordinary they were!

Mom stopped talking and looked at Nastenka with a curious look.

– Mommy, does that mean that I am also the chosen one?– Nastenka asked quietly.

– Each person is valuable in his own right. He has an important task that he must solve, and thus realize himself and benefit the world. And when he is happy with himself, treats himself with an open heart and soul– he is chosen. He has chosen himself to be happy,– replied the mother, gently hugging her daughter.– And then there is less grief and suffering in the world. For whatever wave you launch, it will sound, remember that.

– I'm choosing me, Mommy! I too am opening my heart to myself! I too choose the happiness of being me!

– And that's great! A happy person knows how to inspire others to be happy. After all, happiness is contagious!

– Now I know it's okay to be the black sheep and it doesn't hurt a bit! Thank you, my mommy, you seemed to be the black sheep too! Or maybe you are?– Nastenka looked slyly at her mother and laughed.

– Why, it's already two white crows– not so boring!– Mom picked up the joke.

Nastenka fell asleep happily. Smiling in her sleep, she found the happiness of being herself, so that she could carry this happiness to the world. And when people are happy, the world is happy too!

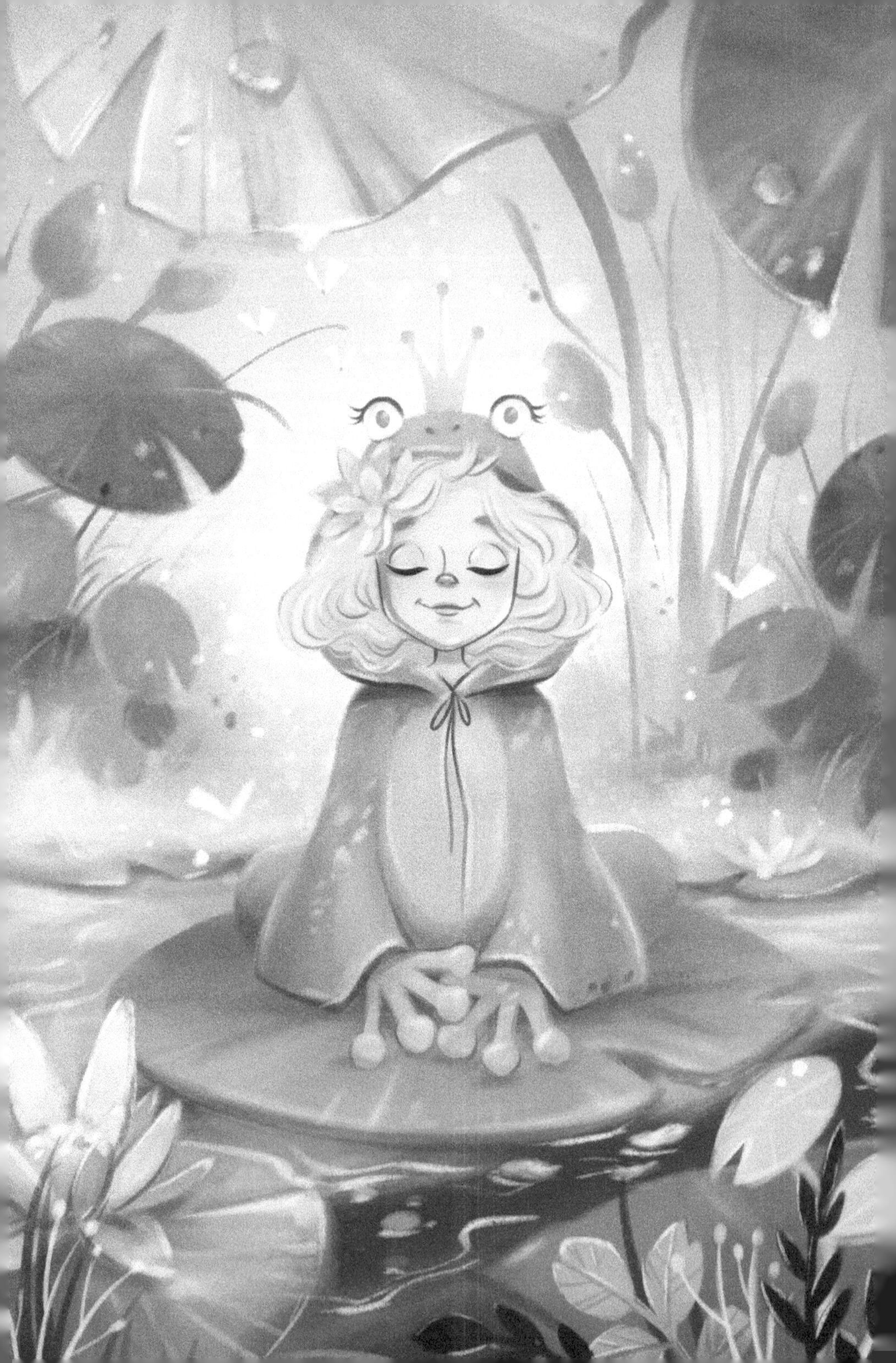

Chapter nine

THERE'S ALWAYS A DEAL TO BE MADE

Nastenka sat by the window, obviously sad about something. Her mother noticed her unusual state at once.

– How was your day, daughter?– Mom asked, pulling clothes out of the drawer. It took longer to get dressed because the cold weather had set in and the snow was covering the ground.

– Tense,– Nastenka grumbled,– I fought with Mishka today.

– And what was this war about?– Mom smiled.

– We couldn't share the new mat in the play area. I was the first to sit on it with my dolls, but he came over and started pushing them off, rolling his cars. We were quarreling so much that we didn't even notice Tatyana Nikolaevna coming over. She didn't bother to sort things out and punished both of us. As a result, we sat in different corners for the rest of the day. Mom, it's not fair!– Nastenka had tears in her eyes.

– A serious task for today,– thought the mother,– I'll have to think about how to help my daughter deal with this situation. After all, as she copes with it now, she will draw on this experience in her life.

– You know what, let's go with you to the ponds. We'll go ice skating, and Daddy will pick us up and we'll go home together. How about that?– Mom asked.

– I don't know, sighed Nastenka. But, after some thought, she agreed.

There were not many people on the ponds. On weekdays there was rarely a large crowd. Taking the skates out of the trunk and put on herself and her daughter, the mother stepped onto the ice.

– Well, daughter, shall we go skating?– she said cheerfully. Movement is life! It speeds up the blood in the body and helps you think. So and roll all your offenses. Ready?

– Ready, Nastenka sighed and confided in her mother. Talking to her always helped Nastenka to understand her thoughts, feelings and difficult situations. Even her dad sometimes joked: "Soon you'll be a professor!"

In the evening, climbing into her bed, Nastenka got ready to listen to another of her mother's stories.

– Mammy, what are you going to tell me about today?– Nastenka asked curiously. The skating trip seemed to have done her good, and she returned home in a good mood.

– Today I'm going to tell you a story about two frogs,– Mom said mysteriously.

– About frogs?– Nastenka was surprised.– Interesting. I'm ready,– Nastenka hugged her mother and got ready to listen.

– A long time ago, two frogs lived in a small pond– a green frog and a yellow frog. They lived happily, each had its own corner, where they built their own houses and sometimes went to visit each other. The pond was beautiful, surrounded by birches and pines. They caught mosquitoes in the reeds and basked in the sun on the leaves of lilies.

One day a lily of amazing beauty grew in the middle of the pond. Its leaf was large and its petals were pink, like the morning dawn on a warm, clear day. The green frog was the first to see this beauty, and decided to climb up on the big dark green leaf, dreaming of how she would greet the dawns and see off the sunsets, enjoying her state as queen of the pond. That was exactly how she envisioned herself in the company of this lily pad.

But the happiness did not last long. As soon as the green frog lay in the morning sunlight, a yellow frog jumped onto the leaf and noticed the lily.

The green frog's anger was boundless. It stomped its hind legs and waved its front legs, trying to kick the yellow frog off the pink lily pad. But the yellow frog was not going to give up, and also defended his right to rest in this beautiful place in the middle·of the pond.

So they quarreled for a week. And it came to the point that they were almost eaten by a white heron, who flew to the pond and saw two mad frogs who did not notice anything around them.

After this situation, the green frog decided that this could not continue and went to the neighboring pond to the wise turtle, who had seen a lot of things in his three hundred years and helped everyone who approached her with advice.

Long or short, the green frog reached the wise turtle. The wise turtle welcomed her warmly, invited her into the house, gave her tea and asked how she was doing. When the guest had rested, the wise turtle asked:

– What brings you to me, green frog?

– A problem brought me to you, wise turtle. You know that I live in a neighboring pond with a yellow frog. We lived together as friends until a big, beautiful lily pad grew in the middle of the pond. One morning I woke up and saw this beauty! I could not remain indifferent and swam to it. Around this lily grew a big green leaf. Climbing on it, I realized how great it is to rest on it, to look at sunrises and sunsets and feel like I was the mistress of the whole space! And just as I was dreaming, a yellow frog jumped on the leaf and literally smashed my dream. I was beyond angry, but I couldn't explain that it was my space, that I was the first to find it. At the moment of our quarrel, we did not even notice the white heron, which flew to our pond and almost ate one of us. So we argue every day about who will sit by the beautiful lily pad. And I came to you to help me solve this problem.

– What is your dream associated with this lily?– asked the wise turtle.

– I want to admire sunrises and sunsets sitting on a leaf next to this magnificent lily! I want to write a poem about this beauty! It inspires me so much that I feel happy when I touch its petals!

– Why is this so important to you?– The wise turtle asked.

– When I look at this beauty, my life is transformed, and every day is filled with meaning,– replied the green frog enthusiastically.

– What would be the best solution to your problem?– The wise turtle asked.

– So that there will be peace in our pond again and I will have an unhindered opportunity to admire the beauty of my lily pad,– the green frog dreamily replied.

– I have a way to help you make the right decision. Are you ready to work hard for your own good?– The wise turtle asked another question.

– Ready,– the green frog said confidently.

The wise turtle swam to the greenest corner of his pond, calling the green frog with him. In this corner there were four beautiful white lilies.

– Now you and I are going to explore this space,– said the wise turtle enigmatically.– I invite you to look at your task from different sides and with different eyes.

– How's that?– wondered the green frog.

– First you will look with your own eyes, then with the eyes of a yellow frog, then with the eyes of an outsider. And at the end of this process, think about what would happen if the situation remained as it is.

– Oh, how interesting,– said the green frog.– You even intrigue me, wise turtle!

So the wise turtle asked the green frog to jump on the first leaf.

– Imagine there is a yellow frog sitting by that very beautiful pink lily pad on the sheet opposite. How do you feel? What thoughts come to mind? What do you want to do?

– Oh, my outrage is unbounded. I'm just furious! I want to throw that self-righteous toad off my sheet!

– Okay, now we know what's happening to you at the moment you're exploring. Now go to the yellow frog leaf, but while you're floating, notice the five water roses, the pistillas. See them.

The green frog jumped into the water and, while swimming to the designated spot, scrutinized the pond in search of the pistillas marked by the wise turtle. As she climbed to the second leaf, she had completely forgotten what she had thought and felt on the first leaf.

– Now,– said the wise turtle,– you are a yellow frog. Just imagine it. And look at the first leaf. A green frog is sitting on it, enjoying the beauty of it, breathing in the fragrance of the beautiful pink lily pad growing in the middle of your pond. What do you, as the yellow frog, feel as you look at all this? What do you think you want to do?

The green frog thought for a moment and then uttered:

– I see a green frog sitting near a beautiful lily pad and rejoicing at the sunrise. I want to sit and watch the sun rise and the new day awaken. The lily leaf is so big, there's enough room for both of us. But I don't agree that this lily belongs only to the green frog. It grew in our pond. And this pond is our home. And we might be able to work things out if the green frog wasn't so squabbling.

The wise turtle was quiet for the green frog to realize a little of what he had seen from the leaf, and then asked him to swim to the third leaf, and while he swam to find five water hyacinths on the pond. When the green frog swam to the third leaf and climbed up on it, the wise turtle gave her the next task:

– Now you're looking at these two frogs from the outside. What's going on between them?

– I see the two frogs arguing over which one of them owns this beautiful pink lily. And they're so caught up in this argument that they don't see the danger they're facing– the white heron.

The wise turtle again suggested that the green turtle jump into the water and swim to the fourth leaf. And now to think about what would happen if everything stayed as it was. The green frog did as the wise turtle told her. And what was her surprise when she realized that if this argument continued, both frogs could become food for the white heron and never again see the beauty of her pond, sunrises and sunsets and, most importantly, her magical pink lily. She also realized that there was no point in fighting and sharing the space of the lily leaf when you could just agree. After all, the yellow frog did not want to quarrel with her.

– What will you do now?– The wise turtle asked her.

– I'll talk to the yellow frog and we'll agree on how and when we can use the space next to the lily pad for the benefit of the two of us.

The green frog thanked the wise turtle for her help and went to her pond. When she reached it, she invited the yellow frog to sit on a pink lily leaf. They had a nice talk, however, as always, and agreed who and when would enjoy the amazing sunrises and sunsets, breathing in the fragrance of the pink lily, and who would at that time watch the pond and report the danger– the white heron, which sometimes visits the pond to have lunch.

From then on, the two frogs lived peacefully and amicably. One of them met the sunrise, the other the sunset, and then they changed places. And while one of the frogs was enjoying the beauty and fragrance of the beautiful pink lily, the other one was making sure that a white heron did not suddenly appear and eat her friend.

The green frog wrote his poem about the lily pad, and the yellow frog painted a picture of that very same lily pad in the beauty of the morning dawn. So they realized their dreams.

Like the wise turtle, the green frogs began to come from neighboring ponds for advice when they had internal disputes and misunderstandings. And she gladly shared her personal experience with them, helping others to find their own solutions.

After a while they had little frogs. They, too, sometimes frolic on the leaf of the rose lily, receiving lessons in beauty and creativity from the older frogs, who gladly passed on their knowledge to them.

These frogs probably still live on their pond surrounded by beautiful pink lilies. That's the story!– Mom finished her story and looked at Nastenka. Nastenka was sitting pensively, going over something in her head.

Finally she turned to her mom and said:
– Mom, I'll make up with Mishka tomorrow. I realized there's room for all of us. We can always make a deal.

– I always knew you were smart, my girl!– Mommy stroked Nastenka's head affectionately.– Now, make yourself comfortable and go to sleep. And may you have wise dreams.

Nastenka closed her eyes and wrapped herself in a warm blanket. Her mother turned off the light in her daughter's room and went to the kitchen. After all, it was also important for her to agree with her husband on several serious issues.

Wise tales for children and adults

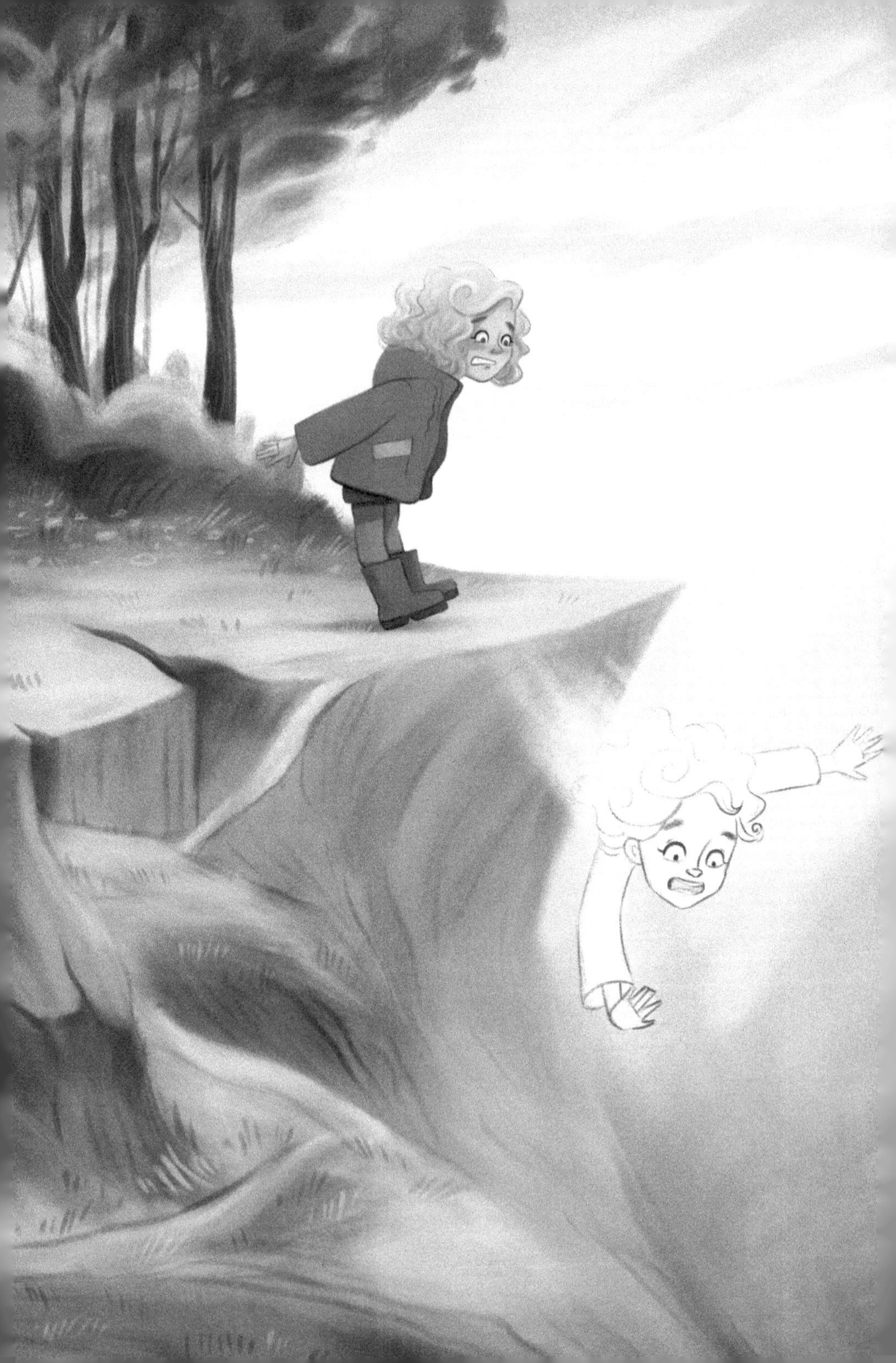

Chapter ten

CAUTION IS NOT AN OBSTACLE

– Mommy, why do people need fear?– Nastenka asked, putting aside the picture book she had recently been given for her birthday.

– Why do you ask that?– Mom asked.

– Yes, I was looking at pictures and remembered how Mishka was very frightened and cried in his sleep today. He woke up the whole group with his crying. And he scared Tatyana Nikolayevna. She was even confused. Why, Mom? To scare her?

Mom looked at her daughter with a smile. She liked talking to her daughter and her curiosity. After all, the more questions, the more answers and the easier it was to live.

– Fear, my girl, is an emotion that arises when you feel danger. Joy occurs when you feel very good, and fear occurs when you are afraid of something or do not understand and do not know what to do with it.

Nastenka thought for a moment, then asked:

– So what, now if I don't understand something, I'm always, always going to feel fear?

– Why always,– Mom smiled. Even though fear lives with a person his whole life, it can be very useful, and it can be tamed. And it can manifest itself in different ways.

– Oh, how interesting!– exclaimed Nastenka.– Tell me, mom!

– If a person is not afraid of anything, he will be constantly exposed to dangers– getting hit by 9a car, falling from heights, eating poisonous food, doing bad things, and many more. Fear is necessary for a person to survive.

– Survive???– Nastenka wondered.– And how is that?

– Here's a counter question. When you and I cross the road, why do you think we cross the road at the crosswalk and when the light is green?

– So you don't get hit by a car.

– That's right. Good girl!– Mom praised her daughter.– After all, if a person runs across the street in the wrong place, there is a chance that sooner or later he may get hit by a car. And a car, running a red light, can hit a pedestrian. People who have a sleeping fear get into such unpleasant situations.

Nastenka thought for a moment. Her mother was carefully watching what was happening to her little girl, so she was in no hurry to tell her more. Finally Nastenka put everything in her head and said:

– So, it is good to be afraid... But then it turns out that I have to live in fear all my life?

Mom laughed and hugged Nastenka:

– Well, why all your life. No, of course not. But fear helps you realize what's good for you and what's not. What you should do and what you shouldn't do. And that's called caution. Sometimes fear can be a beacon that tells you to go where it's scary. And it arises when you have the unknown in front of you and you've never done what's required of you before. Or you want to do it, but you don't know how.

– That's how it is,– said Nastenka, pondering over her mother's words.

– Let me show you examples,– suggested her mother.

– Come on,– Nastenka said excitedly.

– Imagine you're walking on the edge of a precipice.

– Oh, Mom, I'm scared! You can fall down there!– Nastenka exclaimed fearfully.

– There! You feel that? How is your fear helping you?

– He helps me stop and keep my distance rather than getting close to the edge.

– Yes, my Sunshine! That's right. It signals you of danger and keeps you safe. And if it wasn't there, you could fall from a height and get hurt. Nastenka agreed silently, nodding her head.

– Now, I suggest you consider another situation related to this example,– Mom continued.

– Let's consider it,– Nastenka said readily.

– Imagine now that you really need to go downstairs. And it's the only way home. There's no other way. What are you gonna do?

– The only way home? What a problem,– said Nastenka admiringly.– You, mother, are so imaginative!

Mom laughed and hugged her daughter.

– I believe you can do it!

Nastenka sat for about five minutes, searching for different options in her head. Suddenly her eyes lit up and she jumped up:

– Yay!!! I found a solution!

– Which one?– Mom asked.

– I'll be looking for a place where I can get down safely. I saw a movie where tourists were looking for a way down a cliff and found it. There you could hold on to the rocks and the descent was not so steep.

– That's great!– Mom exclaimed.– And who helped you to find

such a solution?– she asked Nastenka.

Nastenka was silent for a moment and then proudly said:

– My caution!

– How did she help you?– Mom was curious.

– She helped me choose a road and showed me the path that was less dangerous. She helped me look for options and find the best one. And I, thanks to her, stay alive and unharmed and make it home! There!

– You're a clever girl,– Mom said admiringly.– Now do you understand why people need fear?

– Yes, Mommy! He helps you find the best solution!

– Yes, my girl! He's helping us. The main thing is that it must not be very strong. Otherwise a person in this state can't do anything. But we'll talk about that next time, okay?

– Okay, Mommy! It's a deal. In the meantime, I'll be friends with caution! I'll go out and be friends!

– Run!– answered her mother and took her for a walk.

This day Nastenka watched everything that was going on more carefully. She did not go close to the swing, realizing that it could hit her. On the slide, she did not go into the crowd, but waited until it was free and it was safe to climb it and roll down with the breeze. Riding a bicycle, she rode on a special bike lane and did not interfere with pedestrians going about their business. When she was out for a walk, she put her little vehicle in the bike parking lot and secured it so that nothing could happen to it. Now she was well aware that caution is not a hindrance, but a good helper in business.

How does your caution help you?

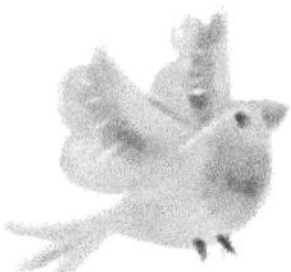

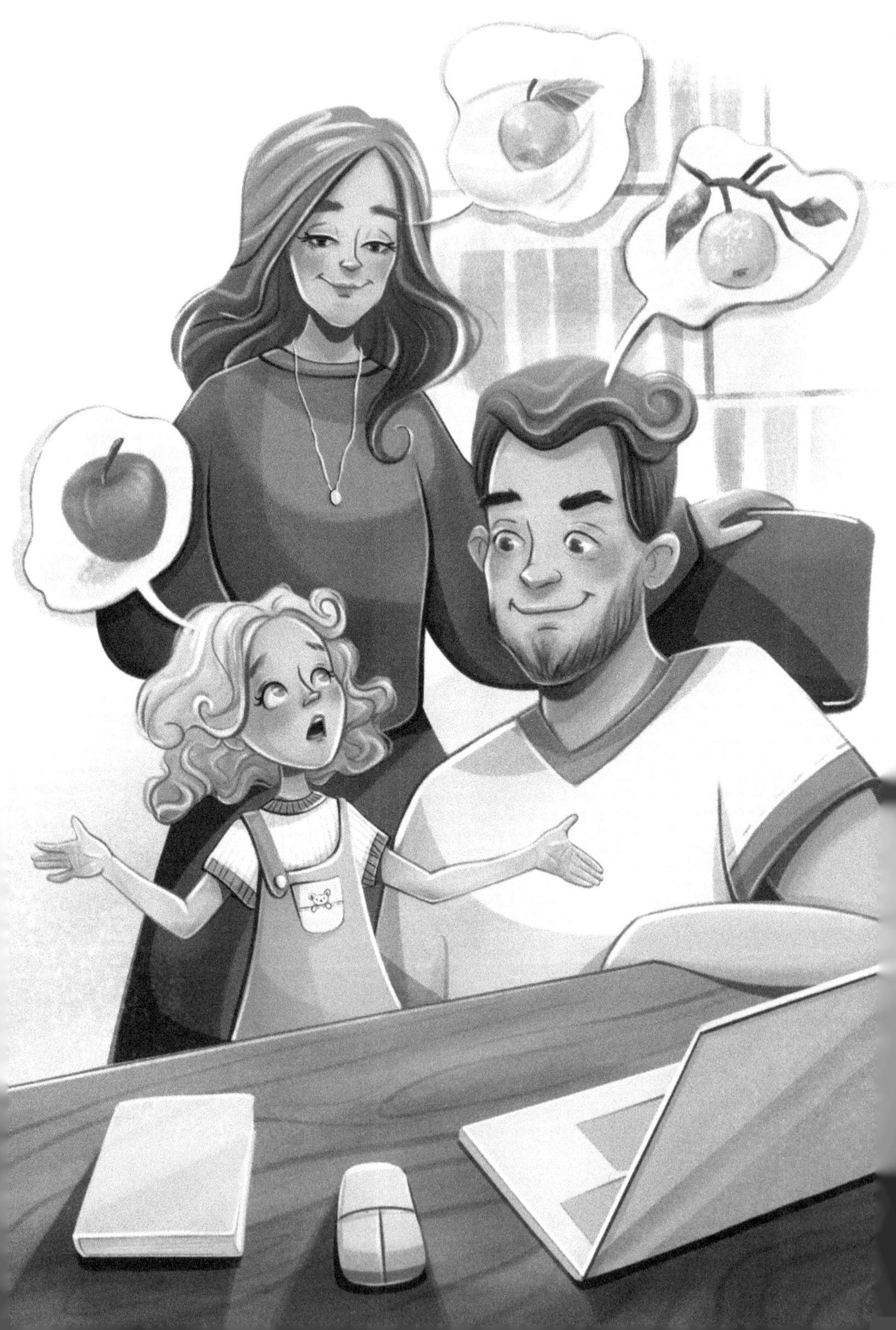

Chapter eleven

HEAR EACH OTHER

– Mommy, why can't people hear each other?– Nastenka asked, climbing onto her mother's lap.

– They can't hear– what do you mean?– Mom asked a clarifying question.

– Well, today we were walking in the garden, and I heard an uncle and an aunt arguing outside the fence. They were talking loudly, proving something to each other, and then the aunt shouted:–You just can't hear what I'm saying!– Why can't he hear? She was talking to him so loudly that even I could hear her.

– That's it,– Mom said,– now I know what you mean. So, are you ready to talk about it?

– Of course, Mom, I'm so interested. I understand that when someone is talking very quietly, you can't hear them. But not being able to hear someone who is talking loudly is a mystery to me.

Mom laughed. She liked her daughter's curiosity. She liked solving life's mysteries with her. She liked to listen to her daughter looking for solutions and finding them. And now a new riddle was born. And it is important that Nastenka learned this life lesson.

– Then imagine you are standing at the staircase leading to the second floor in a house with two floors. There is a position at the bottom– at the beginning of the staircase. There is a second– the platform between the two floors. And there's a third– at the top of the stairs. Can you visualize it?

– Yes, Mommy, I did.

– There is a person standing at each position. Which one do you think can see more than the other two?

Nastenka wondered. At first she thought that the person on top could see more. Then she doubted her quick decision.– He who stands on top cannot see what is going on below,– she thought.

– The one standing at the bottom can't see what's going on up-stairs. And the one standing between the floors only sees the stairs going up and the stairs going down. So what's the result? That no one can see what's going on at the other two?- Nastenka looked at her mother confusedly and told her her guess.

– That's right, my girl, you're a clever girl!– Mommy stroked Nastenka's head.– I just admire the way you are able to explore and make discoveries when we talk to you. Now think and answer, please, can they understand each other without seeing the whole picture of the world opening up before each of them?

– No, of course not,– Nastenka said confidently. None of them sees everything that others see.

– What do you think the reason is?– Mom asked.

– Well they don't have eyes that can get out and explore everything around them! They have to go up or down the stairs to see it all!– Nastenka laughed.

– That's right!– Mom smiled, too.– And what conclusion can be drawn from that?

Nastenka thought for a moment, then answered:

– You shouldn't take offense at someone who doesn't see the whole picture of the world, because everyone has their own little picture. It's like puzzles, isn't it, Mommy? I'm playing with you or Daddy and we're putting puzzles together. And if a piece is missing, the picture doesn't work. You can't see the whole picture.

– That's right, my clever girl!– Mom praised her daughter.

– Wait, Mommy, that's "see"– but what about "hear"? I mean, the lady was yelling: "You can't hear me!"

– It's the same here,– Mom began.– Imagine an apple now. And now describe to me how you see it? What does it look like to you?

Nastenka thought for a moment, imagining an apple:

– It's big, red with yellow stripes, fragrant, sweet... I wanted to eat it so badly!

– Why don't we ask Daddy what kind of apple he has?– Mom suggested it.

– Come on!– Nastenka said cheerfully. She liked this game. Running up to her father, Nastenka hugged him and said mysteriously,– Daddy, imagine an apple.

– I did,– Dad smiled slyly.

– What's it like?– Nastenka said impatiently.

– Big, green, hanging on a branch.

– Wow,– Nastenka said in surprise.– And what, you have a different apple too?– she turned to her mother.

– Yes, daughter, my apple is yellow, sour-sweet, lying in a vase and waiting for me to cut it– smiled Mom.

Nastenka sat in silence for two minutes, realizing something, thinking, examining. Finally, having gathered her thoughts, she said:

– So we can talk about the same thing, but we have different pictures in our heads?

– That's right, my girl.

– And when the different pictures are different, we only see what's in our head and don't see what's in the other person's head?

– That's right.

– And then I'll talk about mine and the other will talk about theirs?

– Here you come to realize another important lesson, daughter. Each person has his own perception and understanding of what is going on around him. And he sees only what he can see, hears only what he can hear, perceives only as he can perceive.

– What do we do now, Mummy? How to hear and understand another person?– Nastenka asked thoughtfully.

– What do you think?– Mom smiled. She didn't want to give her daughter a clue, but let her find the answer to her question.

It took Nastenka some time to realize how to best interact with another person.

– I think,– she said,–we need to understand what apple we are talking about first, and then we can talk about that apple. Right, Mom?

– Yes, daughter,– Mom said affectionately.

– And when it is clear which apple we are discussing, there will be no need to shout and prove that this is not the right apple. And then people will hear each other and understand each other.

– You have found the answer to your question,– the mother hugged her daughter and held her tightly to her chest.– It is very important to learn to understand each other. And this requires a desire to understand, not a desire to prove. When people learn to listen and hear each other, it is easier for them to agree and live in peace and harmony. And if they disagree about something, they can explain what they don't like and together find a solution that suits them.

– That's why you and Daddy understand each other!– Nastenka said enthusiastically.– That's why I'm so smart too!

Mom and Dad laughed. Nastenka laughed too. They were all happy because they could hear and understand each other. And if something is not clear, they can talk to each other and ask questions to reach an understanding. And when there is understanding, life becomes more joyful. It is so interesting to get acquainted with another person's world and share our own. After all, there is something to be surprised and discovered there, too.

How about you?

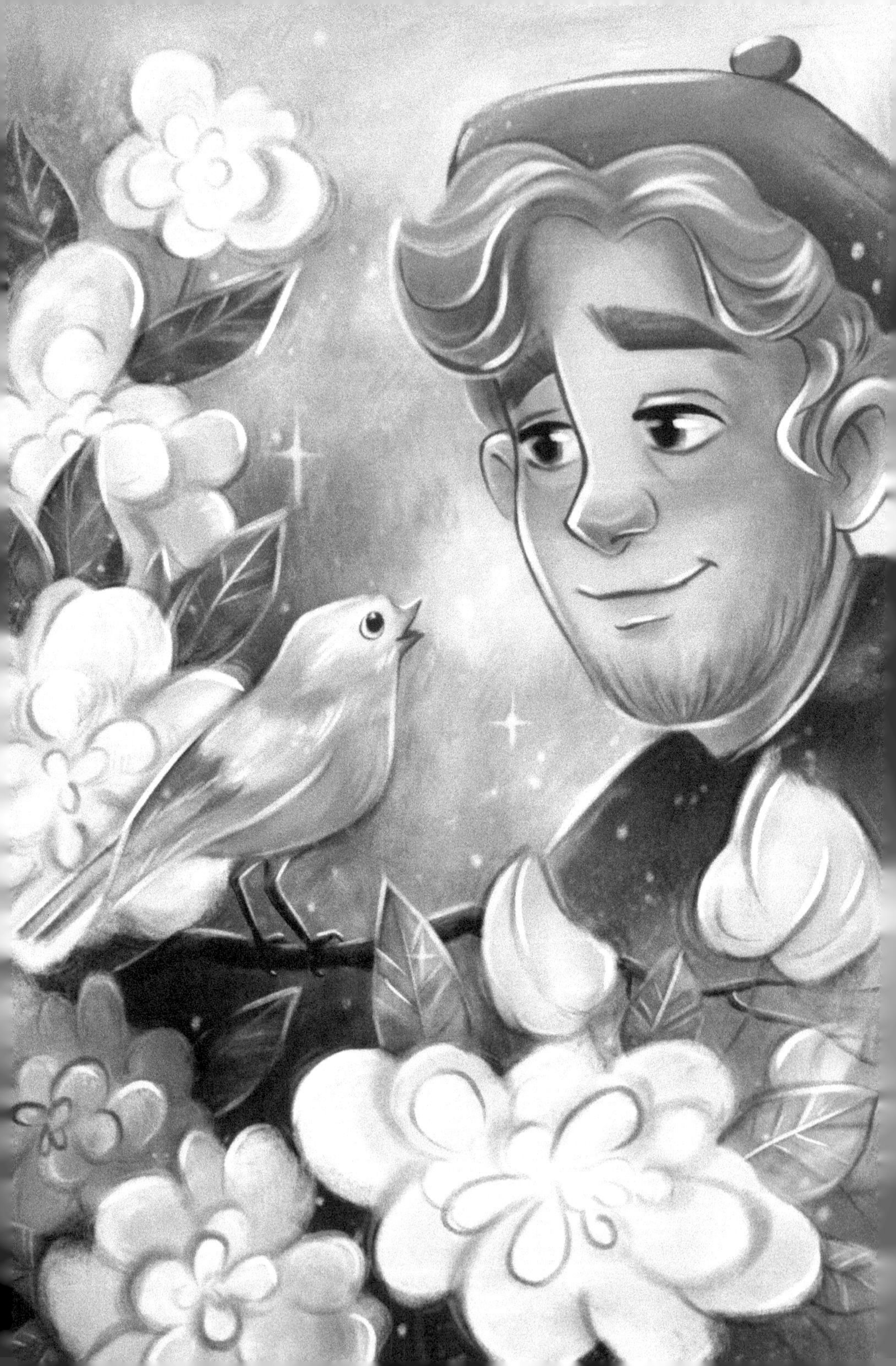

Chapter twelve

A COBBLER WITHOUT BOOTS

Nastenka was going to the dacha. The day before, her mother had made her happy:

– Daughter, as of tomorrow, Daddy and I are on vacation. We have a whole week of vacation ahead of us. And we're going to our cabin in the woods.

– Hurrah!– Nastenka rejoiced. She liked this place very much: forest, lake, walking paths, fresh air, berry meadows. Walk as much as you like! And the neighbors– Grandma Sveta and Grandpa Egor– loved the little girl for her inquisitiveness and immense respect for them.

After putting all her toys in her backpack and saying good night to her parents, Nastenka dived into her bed and, hugging her friend teddy bear, sank into a sweet sleep.

In the morning, as soon as a ray of sunlight touched her cheek, Nastenka woke up, did her exercises, washed her face quickly and ran into the kitchen where her mother was preparing breakfast.

– Mommy, I'm ready!– Climbing on her chair, she solemnly announced.

– Good girl,– said her mother.– It's great when you do everything yourself! You're growing up!

– It's easy,– replied a pleased Nastenka. She liked it when her mother noticed her growing up.

After breakfast, the family went to the dacha. The road, as always, was easy. Everyone was doing his own thing. Daddy skillfully drove the car. Nastenka looked out the window, admiring everything that appeared in it, and her mother read her wise fairy tales, which she wrote down especially for her daughter.

As Nastenka approached the dacha, through the ajar window she heard Grandma Sveta swearing at Grandpa Yegor:

– It's always like that, you help everyone, but you're not enough for the house. It's not for nothing they say– a cobbler without boots!

Mom heard these outrages too and thought: "Looks like this cobbler is definitely going to show up at our house today!"

It didn't take long for her hunch to be realized. As soon as all the things were unloaded and brought into the house, Nastenka ran up to her mother and asked:

– Mom, how can a cobbler be without boots?

– Oh, my daughter, she can!– smiled Mom.– He sews boots for others, but he walks barefoot.

– Why does he walk around barefoot? Is he too lazy to make his own boots?

– It's not laziness, it's just that he often forgets about himself, doing things for others.

– Why should he do everything for others?– Nastenka asked in surprise.

– He is a cobbler, so he sews other people's boots. He earns money and provides for his family,– answered Mother, watching her daughter. She wondered what the next question would arise in Nastenka's mind.

Nastenka thought for a moment. Then she looked at her mother and said:

– What's stopping him from making his own boots?

– I guess he just never thought about it. Or he had, but he hadn't realized that taking care of himself is as important as taking care of others. And if you don't take care of yourself, you won't live long. And you won't help anyone who is sick.

Nastenka thought even more.

– If you want, I'll tell you a story tonight. It's about a man– an artist who was disillusioned with his life and himself.

– Yes!– Nastenka answered happily.– In the meantime I'll go and say hello to our neighbors and look at this cobbler without boots!– and ran off.

In the evening the whole family gathered in the living room. And just as they were about to drink tea, there was a knock at the door. Dad went to open the door, and Nastenka, smiling slyly, looked at her mother.

– Mammy, I told Grandma Sveta and Grandpa Egor that you have a very interesting story about a cobbler without boots, and you know how to help a cobbler make his own boots. They were so interested that they promised to come back in the evening!

Indeed, the neighbors entered the room, followed by a smiling dad. He knew his daughter well, too, and realized that the old men had come for a reason. Nastenka had seduced them with something.

Mom invited the guests to the table, and after a while she began her story.

– In far, far away times, in a mountainous country, there lived an artist. He was a very talented artist. Everyone who looked at his paintings stopped to distinguish where the picture was and where the reality was, so much so that the artist's hand felt everything that his eyes saw, his ears heard, his heart felt. It was as if the Great Master himself was guiding his hand on the canvas. All his paintings were sold as soon as the oil dried on them. And more and more people wanted to own these works of art. But the artist was not happy, as he dreamed of creating his own portrait, but he could not see his reflection, feel himself as he felt everything that surrounded him.

Not far from his house a waterfall flowed. It was beautiful and majestic. And the artist loved to go to it and listen to the music of its flowing waters. Then one day he heard someone inside him whisper:

– Look at yourself in the waters of the waterfall.

The artist was frightened at first, but curiosity took over, and he came to the place where the water flows into a small lake, looked into this rushing stream, and was frightened. An ugly old man was looking at him. A voice within laughed and said:

– Now you're finally gonna get that rubbish out of your head. There's nothing interesting about you!

The artist was very upset and thought that nature had embodied everything she could create that was ugly in him. And the artist decided never to go to the waterfall again and, shutting himself in his cell, began to live out his days, fulfilling only other people's orders and completely forgetting about himself.

And then one day he couldn't paint a picture. It was as if he had forgotten how to do it. Despair seized him. He jumped out of the house and ran to the waterfall so that he could throw himself into its waters and no longer bear the burden of ugliness. But before doing so, he decided to listen to the melody of the waters once more and enjoy the splendor of the beauty of the surrounding nature.

As he sat down on a rock by the waterfall, he suddenly heard a bird singing. The bird's trills were so beautiful that he listened and

forgot all about his intention. After a while he became curious–
where was she hiding? The voice could be heard, but the bird could
not be seen. The artist began to listen and realized that the voice
was coming from somewhere over the water. He came closer to the
waterfall and saw that between the mountain and the flowing water
there was a narrow entrance to a cave, which he had not known
about before.

The artist squeezed through this passage and saw a small platform. And on it was a beautiful bush with beautiful white flowers
that gave off a charming fragrance. And on the very top of this
bush sat a small gray-brown bird and sang. Noticing the artist, it
fluttered its wings and, making a small circle, flew away. The artist
could not take his eyes off this bird, and at one moment his gaze
fell on a wall of water flowing in front of him and recoiled in surprise. A handsome man was looking at him.

Pausing for breath, he approached the waters of the waterfall
again and now scrutinized his reflection. Another voice in his head
said:– Now you know who you really are.

Back home, the artist took a large canvas and painted his portrait. He remembered both his ugliness and his beauty. But he remembered the most important thing– how space can be distorted
when you look into a crooked mirror and see only the outside,
forgetting about the inside.

Since then, the artist's paintings have become true masterpiec-
es. The portrait of the artist now hung in the most prominent place
in his studio. And everyone who came to him was enchanted by
this vision. And a miracle happened– a person discovered beauty
and depth in himself.

The news of this artist spread far beyond the borders of his
country. He had disciples who first learned to paint their own por-

traits and then to fulfill the orders of others. This was the commandment of this Master: through the knowledge of yourself you can see the beauty of the world, and through the knowledge of the world, you can realize your inner beauty. And if you ever want to do something for the world, first do it for yourself. For the true beauty is within.

Mom fell silent, looking around at her listeners.

– Yes,– said Grandfather Egor. He didn't say another word that evening. He only grunted and sipped tea and wattles. Nastenka was also silent.

After seeing the guests off, my mom said:

– Well, my beauty, shall we go to bed?

– Let's go,– Nastenka nodded and, kissing her father, went to her room. When she put her bear friend to bed, she hugged her mother and said:

– Mommy, you are so wise! Now I know that to do as much as I can for the world, I need to become that much myself. So the cobbler needs to make his own boots. And as beautiful and comfortable as possible. And people, seeing this beauty on his feet, will want the same. And since the cobbler has taken care of himself, he will be able to make such boots for everyone. Because his feet are warm!

– You're my sunshine!– Mom hugged her daughter.– Close your eyes, and let you dream of your beauty, which you will then carry to the world. After all, everything is born inside us.

In the morning, having gone to the neighbors' house for raspberries, Nastenka was pleasantly surprised. Grandfather Egor was sitting in a new shirt and repairing the kitchen shelf, and Grandma Sveta was fussing in the summer kitchen– baking pancakes for her husband and singing her favorite songs. Grandfather Egor smiled and sang along to his wife. Happiness settled in their house again.

Nastenka was happy too. After all, it was she, like that bird from the fairy tale, who helped to breathe new life into the walls of the old neighbor's house.

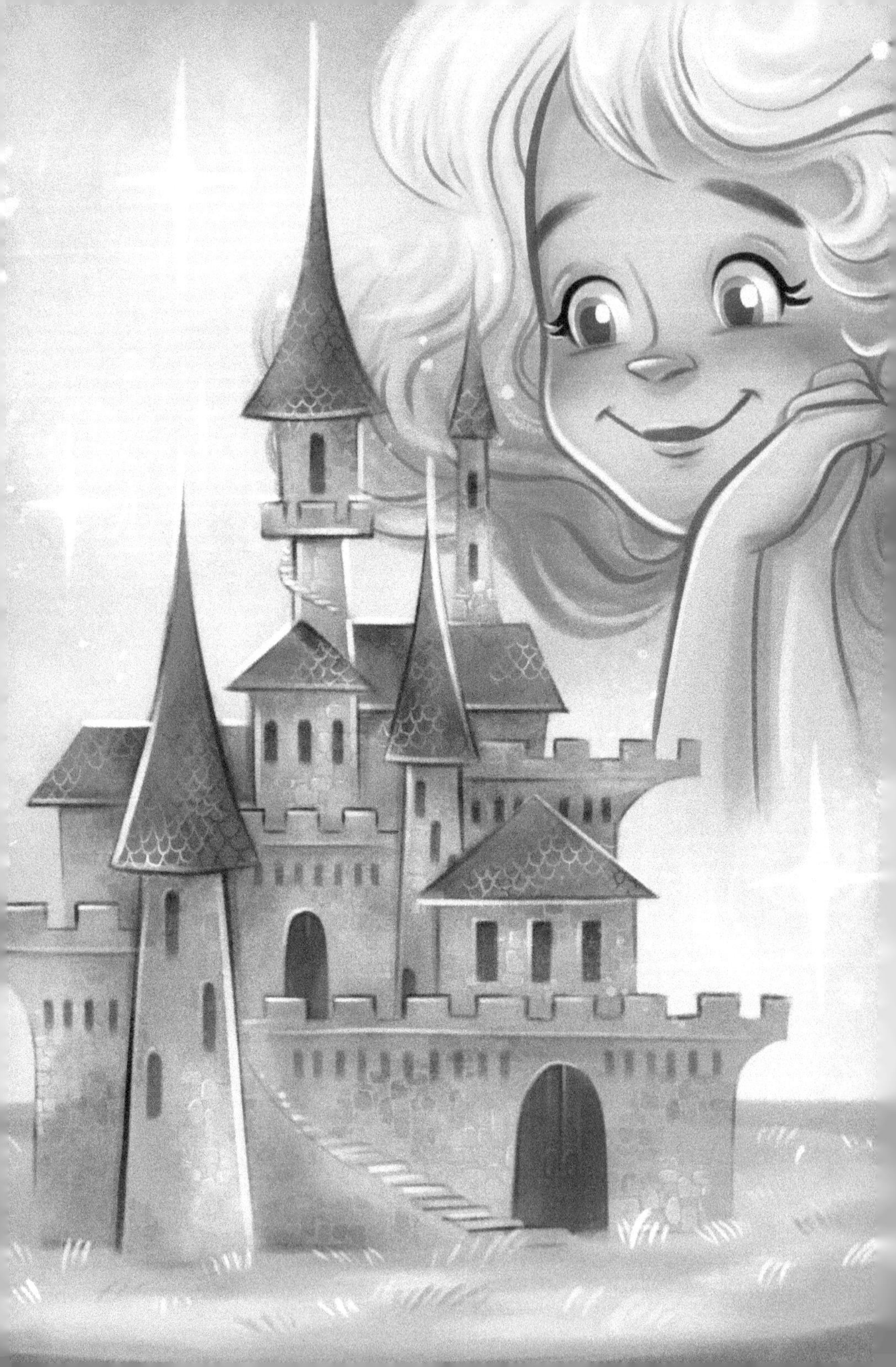

Chapter thirteen

IF IT DOESN'T WORK, DO IT DIFFERENTLY

– Mommy,– Nastenka came into the kitchen, sobbing.

– What's wrong, my dear?– Mom wiped her wet hands and prepared to listen.

– I can't build a house for my doll Mashenka. I have tried a hundred times, and it falls apart and falls apart,– and Nastenka cried at the top of her voice.

– My darling,– the mother hugged her daughter,– I understand why you are worried, and I understand how you feel. You can cry as much as you want. But can I ask you one question?

– I can,– Nastenka said, still sobbing.

– Please tell me, how long does it take you to get over your grief?

– I don't know,– Nastenka replied, raising her eyes at her mother in surprise.– How is that?

– How much longer do you want to cry?– Mom said.

Nastenka thought for a moment and, wiping her tears, replied:

– I don't want to anymore.

– That's right,– Mom exhaled with relief.– No, you can still cry, of course, and I'll feel sorry for you. But maybe we can find a way to make it up to you.

– Fix it?– joyfully, wiping her tears, exclaimed Nastenka.– Yes, Mommy, let's look for it!

– Give me your hand, and let's go look for that magic way that will help you build your house, and Mommy and Nastenka went to the children's room.

There were toys and parts of a toy house scattered on the floor. Her mother suggested that Nastenka take all the toys apart and put them in their places, leaving only the house itself. Nastenka coped with this task quickly and sat down on the carpet to look for a solution to this difficult and, as it seemed to her, impossible task.

– Please show me how you assembled this house,– the mother asked her daughter.

Nastenka tried to put the toy back together, but it fell apart again.

– You see,– Nastenka was about to cry again.

– I get it, daughter,– Mom patted her on the head.– Now let's get to the bottom of this. And first, I suggest you take a good look at the details. What do you see?

Nastenka reluctantly twirled the parts of the house in her hands, but saw nothing that could help her assemble this ill-fated house.

– I don't see anything,– she replied irritably.

– What do you see on the side of these parts?– Mom asked with a sly smile.

Nastenka took one of the parts again, spun it around and suddenly saw some depressions on one part and protruding stripes on the other.

– What's this?– She asked her mom.

– And that's the solution to your riddle,– Mom smiled.

– What does it mean?– Looking at the details from all sides,

Nastenka asked.

– Now look,– said your mother,–you put the pieces side by side and on top of each other, but you didn't fix them, so they fell apart as soon as you tried to place something in the house. Now let's try to connect these protruding strips with the hollows and see what you get.

Nastenka took the cubes and slowly began to insert the protruding part of one cube into the recess of the other. And so the two cubes joined together and did not fall apart. Nastenka jumped with joy:

– Mommy! I did it! Yay!

– You see, my joy, everything worked out!– Mom hugged her daughter and kissed her on the forehead.

– May wise thoughts always come to this clever head!
– And how did you guess that it is possible?– Nastenka asked.

Mom smiled slyly and said:

– I have a golden rule. I'll tell you in confidence, but you can tell everyone later: if something doesn't work, just do it differently.

Nastenka laughed:

– That's a good secret to tell everyone!

– Not only can you, but you should!– Mom said.– If people did not look for ways to solve certain problems, we would have no TV sets, no computers, no lights, no cars, no rockets, and no telephones. There was an American inventor called Thomas Alva Edison. He worked for a long time to create the electric light bulb as we know it today. He tried thousands of ways until he found the one that made it shine for a long time without burning out. And you know what he said?

– What?– Nastenka asked curiously.

– He used to say,–I didn't fail. I just found ten thousand ways that don't work.

– So, like Edison, I, too, have found many ways that don't work? – Nastenka asked admiringly.

– Of course! And he also used to say, – Our greatest weakness is that we give up. The surest way to succeed is to just try one more time,– the mother said, watching her daughter closely.

– Well, mom, you're good!– exclaimed Nastenka.

– What are you talking about?– Mom smiled.

– I'm now going to look for a thousand ways that don't work too!

– How about you combine one with the other?– Mom asked enigmatically.

Nastenka thought for a moment and then answered cheerfully:

– Exactly! I'll look for ways that work, and the ones that don't work will be my discovery too! That's it!

Mom laughed and hugged her daughter gently:

– You see, you've found the wise solution again! Well, you keep building, and I'll go and do the dishes.

After kissing her daughter, her mother went to the kitchen, and Nastenka was engrossed in finding ways to help her assemble a doll's house. Now she had both interest and curiosity, and the strength to do it. She clearly followed her mother's rule:– If you can't do it, do it differently.

CONTENS